Praise for
WHAT THE CEO WANTS YOU TO KNOW

"I learned the universal laws of business in my youth while working at my father's shoe shop. During my career at GE and AlliedSignal I led businesses in sixteen different industries using extensively the ideas discussed in this book. These ideas help simplify complexity and provide a lifetime of value. What the CEO Wants You to Know *is a gem of a book."*

—Larry Bossidy, former Chairman and CEO, AlliedSignal

"This is a book that's been needed for years. Ram Charan shares the secret to finding your way in the business world and making your career more meaningful. Read this book over the weekend or on your next plane trip and you will suddenly see your company and your work in a new light."

—Chad Holliday, Chairman and CEO, DuPont

"Reading this book is like putting on a pair of glasses— suddenly the guts of the business are crystal clear. What the CEO Wants You to Know *is easy to read and the insights are truly energizing."*

—Dave Robino, Vice Chairman, Gateway Computer

Dedicated to the hearts and souls of the joint family of twelve siblings and cousins living under one roof for fifty years, whose personal sacrifices made my formal education possible.

"Finally, a book that shows how business really works. This book captures precisely the kind of business thinking we try to cultivate. It's a great way for leaders at any level to develop their business sense."

—Bob Nardelli, President and CEO, The Home Depot

"Business acumen—Ram Charan's term for using the universal laws of business—is the name of the game today. In this book, Ram takes complex, intimidating concepts and jargon, makes them understandable and creates a set of fundamentals that can be applied to business situations every day, everywhere."

—Lois D. Juliber, COO, Colgate-Palmolive

WHAT THE CEO

WANTS YOU

TO KNOW

WHAT THE CEO WANTS YOU TO KNOW

Using Business Acumen to Understand How Your Company Really Works

RAM CHARAN

CROWN
BUSINESS
NEW YORK

Published by Crown Business, New York, New York. Member of
the Crown Publishing Group.

Random House, Inc. New York, Toronto, London, Sydney,
Auckland

www.randomhouse.com

Crown Business and colophon are trademarks of Random House,
Inc.

Printed in the United States of America

Design by Meryl Sussman Levavi/Digitex

Library of Congress Cataloging-in-Publication Data
Charan, Ram.
    What the CEO wants you to know : using business acumen
to understand how your company really works / by Ram
Charan.—1st ed.
        p. cm.
    1. Executive ability. 2. Middle managers. 3. Success in
business. 4. Corporations—Growth. 5. Industrial management.
I. Title.
HD38.2.C427 2001   00-047403
658.4—dc21

ISBN 0-609-60839-8

20 19 18 17 16 15 14 13

Acknowledgments

This book truly belongs to my siblings and cousins, who practiced the universal laws of business without benefit of formal education, and to the many shopkeepers in villages in India and other countries, who practice business acumen every day of their lives. The real learning came from watching them, as well as from observing some of the best CEOs in the world, to whom I am deeply grateful. It was an incredible learning experience watching Jack Welch, former CEO of GE, over a long period of time cut through to the essence of twelve or more businesses using the same laws of business, each time arriving at different problems and coming up with different answers. Other great CEOs and business leaders have afforded me equal privilege of seeing their minds at work. Those who helped me develop the ideas in this book include Jac Nasser of

Ford, Dick Brown of EDS, Larry Bossidy, formerly of Honeywell, Bob Nardelli of The Home Depot, John Reed, formerly of Citigroup, Lois Juliber of Colgate, Mike Sears of Boeing, Chad Holliday of DuPont, Ivan Seidenberg of Verizon, Bill Conaty of GE, and John Trani of Stanley Works.

I owe special thanks to Jac Nasser, CEO of Ford, from whom I have learned a great deal and who encouraged me to put the universal laws of business in writing so that everyone at Ford could understand them. He and David Murphy, William Swift, Jim Padilla, and Al Ver, also of Ford, provided many incredibly useful insights.

I am very grateful to John Joyce, who was tireless in his efforts to ensure that the book is readable by people of all experience levels, to Leonard Hill and Gary D'Lamater for their input early on, and to Charlie Burck for his comments. Bob Brady and John Galli were also a great resource.

John Mahaney led the charge at Crown Business, providing enthusiastic support and superb editorial guidance throughout the process. I am grateful to him and his colleagues, Chip Gibson, Steve Ross, and Will Weisser, for sharing their expertise so generously and helping bring this project to fruition.

Geri Willigan has been with me on this journey, using her unparalleled ability to take a complex subject and put it in clear, simple language. Her suggestion of ideas, dedication to the project, and professional skills in shaping the book and making it understandable are fantastic. I'm deeply grateful to her.

Contents

Preface

Think back for a moment to your school days. Remember the best teacher you ever had, the one who seemed to know everything about his or her field and had something all the other teachers lacked: the ability to boil down the complex ideas of a discipline— whether it was psychology, economics, or chemistry— so that you really "got it." Other teachers may have had a great depth of knowledge and fancy credentials, but they couldn't make the lightbulb go on in your head. Instead of making something complex seem simple, they did the reverse—they made it more complex and just plain hard to understand.

I've been in the business world some forty years now, beginning when I was a child in my family's small business in India, then working as an engineer in Australia. I then moved to America and taught at both

Harvard Business School and Northwestern University's Kellogg School, and have been advising CEOs and boards of directors at companies large and small around the world. The one thing I've noticed is that the best CEOs—the ones whose companies make money year after year—are like the best teacher you ever had. They are able to take the complexity and mystery out of business by focusing on the core fundamentals. And they make sure that *everyone* in the company, not just their executive colleagues, understands these fundamentals. You could say they have their self-interest at heart, since the company and the CEO are more successful when everyone knows how the business works. But it's not just the CEO who benefits. People feel more connected to their work and have greater satisfaction from their job. And as the company has *profitable* growth—that is, both sales (the "top line") and profits (the "bottom line") increase year after year—there are greater opportunities for people to expand their careers and to make more money.

When you come right down to it, business is very simple. There are universal laws of business that apply whether you sell fruit from a stand or are running a Fortune 500 company. Successful business leaders know them. They have what I call *business acumen*— the ability to understand the building blocks of how a one-person operation or a very big business makes money. You, too, can learn the fundamentals of cash, margin, velocity, return on investment, growth, and customers. You can develop your own business acumen. While these ideas may sound complex, they are not.

Think once more about your best teacher in a subject like chemistry. Once you understood that the atom was made up of protons, electrons, and neutrons, you then had the fundamentals to solve any problem in chemistry. I want to show you that it's the same with business: When you know the fundamentals, you can "get" the basics for how any business works.

My goal in writing this book is to give you the benefit of my experiences over many years in seeing how some of the most successful people in business think and act. You will see the common core of what they do to make their companies and their employees world-class winners. Of course, every business differs to one degree or another, but once you understand the core of any business you will have the framework for understanding your own company.

The best CEOs and the man or woman running the one-person shop think the same way. They know their cash situation. They know which items are profitable and which are not. They understand the importance of keeping their products moving off the shelf (inventory velocity) and they know their customers. What *your* CEO wants *you* to know is how these fundamentals of business work in your company. By investing a couple of hours in this book you'll begin that journey.

RAM CHARAN
Dallas, Texas
January 2001

Part I

BUSINESS ACUMEN

The Universal Language
of Business

What Jack Welch and Street Vendors Share

THE ESSENCE OF BUSINESS THINKING

Chances are that sometime in your life you passed through a city or town where people were selling goods from tables and carts right there on the street. Anywhere you go in the world, you can find street vendors hawking their wares. In Chicago, Mexico City, São Paulo, Bombay, Barcelona, San Francisco, New York. Anywhere.

If you bought something, you probably made your purchase quickly and went on your way. It didn't occur to you to talk to the street vendors about business. After all, what they do is very simple. What could you possibly learn from them?

But if you did talk with street vendors about how they make a living, you would notice something surprising. No matter where they live, what they sell, or what culture they come from, they talk about—and think about—their business in remarkably similar ways. They speak a universal language of business. They practice a universal law of business.

Even more surprising is that the street vendor's language is the same as Jack Welch's language (he's the former chief executive officer of General Electric, named the best manager of the century by *Fortune* magazine) and Michael Dell's language (you've heard of Dell Computer) and Dick Brown's language (CEO of EDS). It's the same as Jorma Ollila's (CEO of the Finnish company Nokia) and Nobuyuki Idei's (CEO of Sony).

In other words, when it comes to running a business successfully, the street vendor and the CEOs of some of the world's largest and most successful companies talk and think very much alike. There are differences, of course, between running a huge corporation and a small shop, and we'll get to those, but the fundamentals, or basics, of business are the same. People like Jack Welch, Michael Dell, and Dick Brown manage and lead large numbers of people in huge, global organizations. They are often referred to as managers or leaders, but they think of themselves as businesspeople first, not unlike street vendors.

I know because I've been permitted to observe some of these business leaders and others like them firsthand. For more than three decades, I have had the privilege of working one-on-one with some of the most successful business leaders in the world, including Larry Bossidy, formerly of Honeywell; Dick Brown of EDS; John Cleghorn of Royal Bank of Canada; Chad Holliday of DuPont; John Reed, formerly of Citigroup; and Jack Welch. I have seen the way their minds work, the way they cut through the largest and most complex issues to the fundamentals of business.

I learned those fundamentals as a child growing up in a small agricultural town in northern India. There I watched my father and uncle struggle to make a living selling shoes from their small shop, a joint family enterprise. With no experience and no formal training, they competed head to head against others in the town who were also trying to eke out a living. My family learned, and over time they built a name brand and earned the trust of the local farmers, who were their customers. Other shops have come and gone, but ours has flourished, and my nephews continue to run the shop to this day.

That shoe shop paid for my education and allowed me to venture far beyond my roots. At the age of nineteen, with an engineering degree in hand, I took a job at a gas utility company in Sydney, Australia. The CEO discovered that I had a nose for business, and I soon found myself devising marketing plans and pricing strategies instead of designing pipeline networks. My interest in business proved to be irrepressible, and that CEO encouraged me to go to Harvard Business School, where I earned an MBA and a doctorate, and where I later taught. Since then, I have had the opportunity to advise dozens of CEOs around the world and to teach business to thousands more.

In my early days of consulting, as I worked with businesses of different sizes, in different industries and different cultures, I was struck by the similarities among successful business leaders. I saw that regardless of the size or type of business, a good CEO had a way of bringing the most complex business down to the fundamentals—the same fundamentals I learned in the family shoe shop.

My experiences over the past few decades have convinced me beyond doubt that the same universal principles, or laws, underlie every business, from the street vendor's business, to the shoe shop, to the businesses run from the executive suites of the *Fortune* 50. The most successful business leaders never lose sight of the basics. Their intense focus on the fundamentals of business is, in fact, the secret to their success. Like the street vendor, they have a keen sense of how a business makes money. This ability to apply the universal laws of business is what I call *business acumen*.

REMEMBER YOUR ROOTS

Many successful CEOs have had experiences early in their lives similar to that of a street vendor, giving root to their business thinking. Larry Bossidy, former CEO of Honeywell, first tested his business acumen in a small shoe store. Think of the challenges a shoe store owner faces. He has to figure out how to attract customers to the shop, what styles, colors, and sizes of shoes to buy, and how to price them. If the shoes aren't selling, he has to decide whether to discount them and by how much to free up cash. He has to put in long, long hours. If he makes a profit, saves money, and has the right people around him, he can grow the business. Every decision matters.

The shoe store is where Larry Bossidy learned the universal language of business. He spoke the same language as vice chairman of General Electric and later at Allied Signal and Honeywell.

Do you speak the universal language of business? Do you understand the fundamental laws that underlie every business? Do you have business acumen?

Chances are, you've built your career in one area of your company, such as sales, finance, or production. These areas, generally known as business functions, are sometimes also called chimneys or silos. That's because most people take their first job at a corporation in one business function and move up within that function as they get promoted. Thus it appears as if they're moving vertically through a chimney or silo.

Such career tracks tend to narrow your perspective and influence the decisions and trade-offs you make every day. What's best for your department or function is not necessarily best for the company as a whole. You may be a top-notch professional—good at marketing or engineering or financial analysis—but are you really a businessperson? Regardless of your job, department, or chimney, you need to develop your business acumen.

As you learn to see your company as a *total business* and make decisions that enhance its overall performance, you will help make meetings less bureaucratic, more focused on the business issues. Time will go quickly, as it does when discussions are constructive and energizing. You'll get more excited about your job because you'll see that your suggestions and decisions help the business grow and prosper. You'll have a greater sense of purpose, and your capacity will increase.

Developing your business acumen will make you feel rejuvenated, like when you were a kid having fun making money for the first time—or like Michael Dell, who instinctively focused on the right things and created tremendous value for shareholders. Fifteen years ago, he was running a mail-order computer business out of his college dorm room. In June 2000, Dell Computer was worth some $130 billion.

When you learn to speak the universal language of business, you can have meaningful discussions with anyone in the company, at any level. You'll tear down the walls that separate you, a functional chimney person, from those well-dressed senior executives and MBAs who speak a language you may not understand. You'll feel more connected to your company and your work. And the range of opportunities open to you will expand.

Use this book to learn the language of business. Then put the book aside and practice until the fundamentals of business become instinctive, as they are for the street vendor. You'll discover the common sense of business, and you'll be on your way to developing business acumen.

THE STREET VENDOR'S SKILL

How does a street vendor hawking fruits and vegetables in a small Indian town make a living? Someone with a $75,000 education and an MBA might say "Anticipate demand." But the street vendor in India doesn't know the buzz words. He just has to figure out what to buy that morning—what quantity, what quality, and what assortment of fruits and vegetables—based on what he thinks he can sell that day (his *sales forecast*).

Then he has to figure out what prices to charge and be nimble enough to adjust prices as needed during the day. He doesn't want to carry the fruit (the *inventory*) home with him. If it begins to decay, it will be of less value tomorrow. Another reason why the vendor doesn't want anything left over is that he needs the *cash*. All day long he has to weigh whether to cut prices, when to cut them, and by how much. If he is indecisive or makes a wrong trade-off, he may lose out.

It is no different in companies. Say the Federal Reserve (the Fed) increases interest rates. Demand for automobiles might suddenly drop, and automotive companies might not be able to adjust their production levels quickly enough. They might end up with more inventory than they need. It would then take heroic efforts to dispose of the inventory and collect the cash. That's when consumers would start seeing TV commercials telling them that one of the car companies is offering cash rebates. Rebates and increased spending on advertising hurt profits. Also, such selling approaches can begin to cheapen the image of the brand. Companies sometimes endure those negative effects because they need the cash.

Each morning, the street vendor sets up his cart. He puts the best-looking fruit in the front (retailers call this *merchandising*). He watches the competition—what they're selling and for how much. And the whole time, he's thinking about not just today but also tomorrow.

If he has trouble selling his produce, he might have to cut the price (increase the value to the customer) or rearrange the display or yell louder (advertise) to attract attention to his stand. Maybe tomorrow he'll find a better price at which to buy or he'll change the assortment of fruits and vegetables (the *product mix*). If something doesn't work, he adjusts.

How does he know if he's doing well? When he has cash in his pocket at the end of the day. Everyone understands *cash*, money in the pocket. Every language has a word for this. The street vendor constantly thinks about cash—does he have enough cash, how can he get more cash, will he continue to be able to generate cash?

What happens to the street vendor who doesn't have cash at the end of the day? It's misery all over. The tension in the family is almost unbearable. The wage earner loses face. And yes, it's true; in India, his family may not have enough to eat. Such circumstances put the mind into sharp focus. But whether the street vendor realizes it or not, his subconscious is pondering something deeper. How will he buy goods for the next day? He needs cash to stay in business.

So do companies. You hear all the time about companies that are strapped for cash. They may have produced too many things that didn't sell and the cash got absorbed in inventories. Or they invested money in a plant that's too big and the company can't generate enough money from it. Or the company sold its products on credit to distributors or retailers and got paid late or not at all. When companies can't generate enough cash, they often borrow it. If they borrow heavily and don't correct the problem that created the need in the first place, they have trouble repaying the loans. Some end up filing for bankruptcy, so-called Chapter 11.

Back to the street vendor. How vendors buy fruit varies from country to country. In India, when personal cash savings are hard to accumulate, the vendor may borrow cash to purchase fruit in order to make some more money. To make a living, he has to make enough money to pay back what he borrowed, with some left over.

Every time he sells a melon, he makes just a little bit of money. His profit, the difference between what he pays for the fruit and what he sells it for, is very low. His *profit margin*—the cash he gets to keep as a percentage of the total cash he takes in—is around 5 percent. (Different companies have different terminology for this basic idea. Some call it *return on sales* or *operating margin*. You need to know what it is called in your company. But what's important is the idea, which I'll explain more fully later.)

Let's say our street vendor borrows 400 rupees (Rs 400, which is about $10). He uses the money as a deposit on Rs 4,000 worth of fruit. The fruit is his only asset. If he sells all Rs 4,000 worth of fruit at a 2 percent profit margin (after deducting all expenses and his salary), he will make a profit of Rs 80. In other words, he used his Rs 400 asset to make Rs 80, so his *return on assets* is 20 percent.

Can the street vendor raise his prices to make more profit? Only so much. If his price is too high, his customers will go to another vendor. Can he find a way to pay less for the fruit? If he buys fruit that's overripe, his customers will know the difference. Maybe some kinds of fruit are more profitable than others. Should he sell only the most profitable ones?

In the automotive business in the early 1990s, Ford gained a decisive financial advantage over General Motors by changing its product mix ahead of the competition. Ford was quick to recognize the American consumer's increasing desire for sport utility vehicles and light trucks. While continuing to offer a full range of vehicles, Ford shifted some of its production from cars to SUVs and trucks, which are more profitable than cars. It won the leading market share in North America in these product areas, despite the fact that GM was bigger.

The street vendor has many realities to deal with. If he makes the wrong judgment repeatedly, he will find it hard to make a living. If he doesn't give his customers a fair deal, they will not return and he will develop a bad reputation. If, on the other hand, he gives people a good deal every time, he builds their trust and loyalty to his brand. He has to be *consumer focused.*

LEARNING FROM THE STREET VENDOR

Running a one-person business may seem simple, but it requires many decisions. These judgments are made intuitively—and without the benefit of computers, sophisticated forecasting techniques, or off-site meetings at expensive resorts! The skill and business acumen of the street vendor is passed down from generation to generation in cities and villages around the world. Children listen to their elders at the dinner table, participate in the business, and then go out on their own. They intuitively come to understand how the total business operates.

My experience growing up in India is typical of how children learn about business. To this day, I recall how every evening around nine o'clock my male cousins and I followed my father and uncle home from their shop and gathered on the rooftop to escape the sweltering heat below. We discussed the day's events—which customers came or didn't come, what sold or didn't sell, whom we needed to collect money from the next morning, and what the two most prosperous shops in the village were doing *(best practices)*.

I saw my elders struggle every day to build relationships with customers and make the right adjustments in the mix of shoes they sold and the prices of the shoes. Every time they made a sale, the competitor, whose shop shared a common wall with ours, tried to persuade the customer to return the shoes to us and buy from him. It was hand-to-hand combat. Yet at the end of the day, the family made ends meet. Although we didn't use fancy terminology, we were learning the basics of money making, developing our business acumen, and creating value for *shareholders* (the family members). That value, by the way, included my formal education and the many opportunities that followed.

You probably are not a street vendor or a shop keeper. But whether you are just beginning your career or are an executive at the top of a silo, there's much you can learn from the street vendor, who knows every aspect of his business—product, sales, customers, profit margin, return on assets. You too can develop the business acumen to understand, at the most basic level, what it takes for a business to make money.

2

Every Business Is
the Same Inside

CUTTING THROUGH TO CASH, MARGIN,
VELOCITY, GROWTH, AND CUSTOMERS

Business acumen requires understanding the building blocks of money making. Think back to how you learned physics or chemistry. First you had to understand the parts of an atom: electrons, protons, and neutrons. Once you understood the parts and how they interact, you were ready to develop your knowledge. It's the same in business.

When two businesspeople talk, whether or not they are in the same industry, whether or not they talk openly, they always try to gauge: Is her business making money? How is her business making money? How is the money making likely to change? Businessmen and businesswomen have an insatiable desire to cut through the complexity to the fundamental building blocks of money making.

Money making in business has three basic parts: cash generation, return on assets (a combination of margin and velocity), and growth. True businesspeople understand them individually as well as the relationships between them. Add consumers to these three parts of money making—cash generation, return on assets, growth—and you have the core, or nucleus, of any business.

Cash generation, margin, velocity, return on assets, growth, and customers: Everything else about a business emanates from this nucleus. Does the business generate cash and earn a good return on assets? Are we retaining customers? Is the business growing? If so, common sense tells you that the business is doing well. A large, complex company will eventually falter if this core is not right.

Don't let your formal education or the size of your company obscure the simplicity of your business. Think like the street vendor. Cut through to the nucleus of the business. If your business shows deterioration in one or more of the basic components of money making, use common sense to fix it. If you do, you are on your way to thinking and acting like a true businessperson and a successful CEO!

CASH GENERATION

Cash generation is one of several important indications of money-making ability. An astute businessperson wants to know, Does the business generate enough cash? What are the sources of cash generation? How is the cash being used? Any businessperson who fails to ask these questions and figure out the answers eventually stumbles.

Cash generation is the difference between all the cash that flows into the business and all the cash that flows out of the business in a given time period. Cash flows into the corporation from sources like the sales of its product or services that are paid for in cash and payments by customers for previous sales made on credit. Cash flows out of the business for items like salaries, taxes, and payments to suppliers.

The street vendor conducts all his business on a cash basis. His customers pay him in cash, and he pays his suppliers in cash the same day. For him, cash and income are one and the same. But most companies extend credit, so cash and income are different. They make a sale now but collect the money later. They buy something now and pay for it later. They have *accounts receivable* (money customers owe them) and *accounts payable* (money they owe their suppliers). The timing of these payments affects cash generation.

Cash generation can be a problem even for the largest companies. Chrysler ran out of cash in the early 1980s; Volkswagen faced a cash crisis in the late 1980s; and Montgomery Ward ran out of cash several times in the past fifty years.

One of the clearest examples of problems with cash generation was in—would you believe?—a management consulting firm. The senior partners of the firm had borrowed a lot of money to buy the company and therefore needed a lot of cash every month to make the interest payments. At one point in 1998, it became clear that they were running out of cash. The only solution, it seemed, was to sell a piece of the business, which of course would diminish the value of each partner's share.

Then just before the deal was struck, the partners had an insight that saved their stake in the business. They discovered that the firm had lost discipline in its billing procedures. Consultants were not billing clients in a timely way, and clients were sometimes delaying payment. Accounts receivable—money clients owed the firm—was 84 days instead of the 45-day industry average. The firm had nearly twice as much money waiting to be collected as it should have had. In the meantime, the firm was continuing to pay salaries and travel, administrative, and office expenses to keep the business running.

The firm addressed the billing problems, and the cash situation dramatically improved. Bonuses were restored, the firm bought the new information system it sorely needed, and the partners retained their full ownership of the business.

Cash gives you the ability to stay in business. It is a company's oxygen supply. Lack of cash, decreasing cash, or consumption of cash spells trouble, even if the other elements of money making—such as profit margin and asset velocity—look good.

Every company is required to show in its annual report where the cash came from and went during the year and what the net cash generation was for that period. Do you know whether your company is a net cash generator? And why it is or isn't? If it is not generating cash, is this because your management is investing in activities to grow the company, or because you have too much inventory that you're not selling?

If you work for a large company, does your division generate cash? Does your business in, say, Brazil consume or generate cash? Sometimes you hear a division president say, "I'm managing my division for cash, not growth." That's shorthand for what top management expects from the division. Management might decide, for example, to use the cash from a division serving a slow-growth market (growing, say, 1 to 2 percent a year) to fund the R&D (research and development), marketing, and plant expansion of another division in a fast-growth industry.

Or sometimes a company is owned by family members who depend on the business as their main source of income. Such companies are often "managed for cash," meaning that the family expect the business to generate money to meet their immediate needs.

Everybody Counts

Most people can understand cash on a small scale, in their own everyday life. If the bills are due before the paycheck arrives, what happens? In a large company, however, some people lose sight of cash. Many think that's the responsibility of the finance department.

But everyone in a company must be aware that his actions use cash or generate cash. A sales representative who negotiates a 30-day payment from a customer versus 45 days is cash wise. The company gets the money sooner, and that frees up cash—that is, makes the cash available to use for other things. A plant manager whose poor scheduling results in the accumulation of a lot of inventory consumes cash.

The decision to build a new plant clearly affects cash generation. Take the case of Miller Brewing Company. Philip Morris purchased Miller in 1970 and set the regional brewery onto a major growth trajectory. Market share rose quickly from 8 percent to nearly 20 percent. Encouraged by this momentum, management built a $460 million brewery so the company could increase production as market share continued to climb. But before the new plant was up and running, the company's archrival, Anheuser-Busch, made some aggressive marketing moves and stopped Miller in its tracks. Miller's market share did not increase as hoped for, the plant opening was delayed several years, and cash generation went negative. Cash flowed out of the company to build the plant, but no additional cash flowed in because sales did not increase as planned.

Even mailroom clerks have a role to play in cash generation. They sort and deliver the mail—letters, bills, checks. Checks!

Let's say the mail arrives Friday morning. The mailroom might not sort and deliver it until that afternoon. Maybe the checks don't get to the right department until 4:30 P.M. By then, the people in accounts receivable are getting ready to go home. They'll open the mail on Monday. When does the check turn into cash? Three days after it gets to the bank.

Also think about when the mail gets sent. In many companies, invoices prepared after 2 P.M. on Friday aren't sent out until Monday morning. By getting the invoices in the mail before the end of the day Friday, the company receives payments two days sooner and improves its cash situation. So lots of people keep the cash flowing, including the men and women in the mailroom.

In recent years, some very smart businesspeople

have figured out highly efficient ways to generate cash. Many of these efforts focus on inventory, which ties up cash. Look at Amazon.com, one of the pioneers of Internet-based retailing. It's the on-line bookstore, open twenty-four hours a day, seven days a week. When Amazon.com first started out, it did not carry inventory. That gave it a huge cash advantage over traditional booksellers, which had lots of books in lots of book-stores and warehouses. Amazon.com would receive book orders on-line and ship them from someone else's distribution facility to the customer. Amazon.com got paid by the customer's credit card company when the books were shipped, but it didn't pay for the books until a few weeks later. It generated cash and used that cash for marketing, which resulted in more sales. (Amazon.com has since changed its business approach. It built warehouses and now maintains inventory.)

Similarly, Dell Computer, which sells personal com-puters directly to customers, gets paid by credit card *when* the PC is ordered and *before* the customer receives it. However, Dell pays its suppliers (those who make the individual components of the computer) in the usual 30 days after receiving the parts. It maintains just 6 days of inventory. In a given period, Dell has more inflow of cash than outflow. Thus the more it grows, the more cash it generates. Some say that Dell is a cash machine.

The "new economy" companies like Dell aren't the only ones that generate cash. Many "old economy" com-panies, such as GE, McDonald's, and United Technologies, are cash generators. GE, for example, has consistently generated cash for ten years. By making its manufacturing facilities and flow of production more efficient, it has reduced its inventory needs and increased its manufacturing capacity without having to build new factories.

Smart businesspeople know that generating cash can help grow the business. Invested wisely, cash improves the company's money-making ability. There's a psychological component to cash: When a company has its own cash rather than borrowed money, senior managers are more inclined to make bold investments that have greater potential rewards.

RETURN ON ASSETS

You might think that making money simply means making a profit—"buying low and selling high." But there's more.

Regardless of the size or kind of business, you're using your own or someone else's money to grow. You borrow from a bank or use your savings. That money represents your investment, or your *investment capital*. If you inherit the business, the "investment" is given to you.

Your investment then takes one form or another, whether it be products (inventory), a small store and some shelving (plant and equipment), or an IOU from a customer who took something home (accounts receivable).

The things you've invested in are *assets*. The assets of an automobile manufacturer include the factories and assembly plants, office buildings, computer systems, and inventories of sheet metal, paint, and components.

These are *tangible assets* you can see and touch. The big items, like buildings and machinery, that are not expected to be sold are sometimes called *fixed assets*.

Even if your company is not a manufacturing business, you have investments. In a service business such as insurance, there are no parts inventories or manufacturing machinery. But your cash is tied up in other ways. Government regulations require insurance companies, for example, to maintain a certain amount of cash on reserve so they can be sure to pay customers' claims. That cash reserve is an asset.

Find out the tangible assets in your company. A person with great business acumen will wonder how much money you are able to make with those assets. What kind of money is being returned to you through their use? In short, what is your *return on assets,* your *ROA?* Are you making enough of a return on those assets?

Some people would rather talk about *return on investment* or *return on equity* (*equity* is the money shareholders have invested in the business). The differences between these things are technical. It's the same concept for all of them: How much money are you making with your investments, or with the money shareholders have invested in the company?

You don't need an MBA (master's degree in business administration) to understand the idea of return on assets. Let me prove the point. Many years ago, I took a group of MBA students to an open-air market about eight miles from Managua, Nicaragua. There, merchants and peasants (almost all women) sold all sorts of things, from pineapples to shirts and necklaces.

We approached a woman selling clothing from a small cart, and I asked her how she got the money to pay for her merchandise. She said she borrowed it, for 2.5 percent interest a month. A student did some quick math—2.5 percent multiplied by 12 months—and announced that the interest rate was a whopping 30 percent a year. She corrected him. Accumulated, or compounded, month to month, the interest rate was more like 34 percent a year.

How much profit did she make? Just 5 percent. So how could she survive borrowing money from the loan sharks? We had to ask.

Annoyed by the stupidity of the question, she propped her right elbow on her left hand and made several sweeping circular motions through the air. Her gesture meant rotation—rotation of inventory, rotation of stock, turning the stock over.

She knew intuitively that earning a good return had two ingredients—profit margin and velocity. If she sold a shirt for $10, she made just 50 cents profit. To pay interest on the loan and to restock her cart, she had to sell her wares again and again every day of the week. The more quickly she sold, the more "5 percents" she accumulated.

The word *velocity* describes this idea of speed, turnover, or movement. Think of raw materials moving through a factory and becoming finished products, and think of those finished products moving off the shelf to the customer. That's velocity.

Or picture a grocery store whose owner has made little investment in the shop itself and sells for cash only.

All the assets are in the form of inventory. Does the grocer empty her shelves and replace the goods each day, or does it take a week to clear the shelves? The first scenario has higher inventory velocity than the second. For many companies, inventory velocity is a very revealing number.

Some people use the term *inventory turns* to describe inventory velocity. How many times does the inventory turn over in a year? Wal-Mart has 360 inventory turns in toilet tissue. That means the entire inventory of toilet tissue is sold almost every day. Each day, Wal-Mart gets back the money it spent on its inventory of toilet tissue, plus some profit. That's a terrific use of shelf space.

Whatever the assets, figuring out asset velocity requires some simple arithmetic: your total sales for, say, a year divided by total assets. If you want to look at inventory velocity, divide total sales by total inventories. But forget the math. Get the *idea* of velocity. Things must move through a business to the customer— the faster, the better.

How long is it from the time an order comes in to the time it is delivered to the customer? How long from the time a company receives raw materials and parts to the time finished product is being sold out of the retail stores, warehouses, or distribution centers?

In the United States it takes an average of 72 days from the time a new car is ready to be shipped from the plant to the time it reaches the consumer. That whole time, the money used to buy the parts that went into the car is tied up. The manufacturer can't get any of it back to use for another purpose until the car reaches the consumer. If the car gets to the consumer sooner, the manufacturer has a lot less money tied up in a product that's sitting on a railroad track or car carrier. That's what I mean by moving faster. That's velocity.

The faster the velocity, the higher the return. In fact, return on assets is nothing more than profit margin multiplied by asset velocity. This is a universal law of business that can be written simply:

$$\text{Return} = \text{Margin} \times \text{Velocity}$$
$$\text{or}$$
$$R = M \times V$$

This is not financial jargon. $R = M \times V$ is a tremendously useful business tool that is well worth memorizing. The result, R, is stated as a percentage—8 percent return, 10 percent return, 15 percent return—a single number that can be used for comparison.

When it comes to gauging the health of the business, a good CEO is not so concerned about precision. She uses return on assets (or a similar measure) to get a sense of the business. Is it better than last year and the year before that? Is it better than its competitors? Is it where it should be? The best companies have a return on assets greater than 10 percent after tax.

Making Margin Meaningful

Throughout this book, we use the term *margin* to refer to *net profit margin* after taxes. That is, the money the company earns after paying all its expenses, interest payments, and taxes. These expenses include all the costs associated with making and selling the product as well as running the business, making interest payments on any loans, and paying income taxes.

Gross margin, from which net profit margin is derived, is also critical to understanding the fundamental anatomy of the business. Gross margin is calculated by taking the total sales for the company or a product line and subtracting the costs *directly* associated with making or buying the product or service. Say the shopkeeper buys 1,000 pairs of shoes at $30 a pair and sells them for $50. His total sales are $50,000 (1,000 pairs × $50 each = $50,000). The costs directly associated with the shoes *(the cost of goods sold)* are $30,000 (1,000 pairs × $30 each = $30,000). We can use those two numbers (total sales and total costs) to figure out the gross margin.

$50,000 total sales − $30,000 cost of goods sold
= $20,000 gross margin

Out of the $50,000 the shopkeeper collected for his shoes, he has $20,000 above and beyond what it cost him to acquire and sell the shoes. His gross margin is 40 percent, since $20,000 is 40 percent of $50,000.

Many businesspeople and investors track gross margin because it provides clues about important changes that are affecting the nature of the business. For example, if your gross margin goes from 52 to 48 percent, you have to ask why. Is it costing more to produce your product, or is competition forcing you to lower prices while costs are staying the same? In the early days of the personal computer, the PC industry enjoyed gross margins approaching 38 percent. Then came the era of

R-O-What?

Some companies use slightly different measures of return. Instead of looking at return on assets (ROA), they look at return on investment (ROI) or return on equity (ROE). Don't be intimidated by the acronyms. All of these measures are similar in concept. They tell you how much money is coming into your business from the use of your assets, from the investments the business has made, or from the investment shareholders have made in the company (equity).

Calculating ROA, ROI, and ROE is not hard. Start with the universal formula $R = M \times V$, where R means return, M means margin, and V, velocity.

For *return on assets,* multiply margin by velocity of assets (velocity of assets is sales divided by assets). Let's work it through for a company that has a 5 percent profit margin, $10 billion in sales, and $2 billion in assets:

$$R = 5 \text{ percent} \times (\$10 \text{ billion}/\$2 \text{ billion}).$$

The return on assets, ROA, is 25 percent.

For *return on investment,* multiply profit margin by velocity of investment (velocity of investment is sales divided by investment). Assume this company has a 5 percent profit margin, sales of $10 billion, and total investments of $5 billion:

$$R = 5 \text{ percent} \times (\$10 \text{ billion}/\$5 \text{ billion}).$$

The return on investment, ROI, is 10 percent.

For *return on equity,* multiply profit margin by velocity of equity (velocity of equity is sales divided by equity). Use a 5 percent profit margin and $10 billion sales, and assume $1 billion in shareholders' equity (this excludes money the company may have borrowed from a bank):

$$R = 5 \text{ percent} \times (\$10 \text{ billion}/\$1 \text{ billion}).$$

The return on equity, ROE, is 50 percent.

intense price competition. The price of a PC fell dramatically, which shaved gross margin by some 20 percentage points. To survive, PC makers had to change their entire business approach by outsourcing components manufacturing, cutting costs, and increasing velocity.

Or it could be that gross margin is declining because the customer mix is changing. You're selling more products that have lower margins and fewer of the high-margin goods. Is the trend going to accelerate?

Making Velocity Meaningful

Many people focus on profit margin, but they overlook velocity. Here's what makes successful CEOs different from many other executives: They think about both margin and velocity. This dual focus is the centerpiece of business acumen.

Velocity is important to every company. First consider those that have a lot of fixed assets—factories, machinery, or buildings. Take, for example, a company like AT&T. It has a huge investment in wires, cables, satellites, and microwave towers. With prices for long-distance voice calls falling and margins shrinking, the only way to improve the return on assets is to focus on velocity. AT&T has to increase the amount of money made with those assets. That's why you've seen it and other telecommunications companies desperate to increase their sales (revenues) and, like the street vendor, trying to get the right product mix. AT&T's CEO, Michael Armstrong, publicly stated that revenue growth would be AT&T's highest priority for 2000, 2001, and 2002.

Companies that have low fixed assets can have a return on assets in the triple digits. Dell, for example, is essentially an assembler of computers. It does not manufacture a lot of component parts. Thus Dell doesn't have to own a lot of buildings and manufacturing equipment. For the year 1999–2000, Dell's return on invested capital (the measure Dell uses and believes best measures its efficiency) was a whopping 243 percent! That's twice what it was the year before.

Dell didn't get to such a high return because it can command high margins. It got there because Michael Dell figured out velocity. He saw that other low-margin businesses, like mass merchandising, were earning a respectable return with margins of around 3 to 4 percent. That got him thinking about how they did it, and he discovered the other part of the $R = M \times V$ equation.

Can you guess Dell's *inventory* velocity? It was about 50 for the year ended January 28, 2000. Dell has very little inventory because its computers are made to order. That is, they are assembled to each customer's specifications and delivered in less than a week. Now senior executives of companies like United Technologies and Pratt & Whitney are visiting Dell to learn how to produce and deliver on demand with low inventories.

As you hone your business skills, think hard about return on assets and its basic ingredients of velocity and profit margin. Look at your own company's return on assets. If you don't think it's adequate, press for ways to improve it. Even if you don't have all the answers, you can help by asking the right questions: How does your company's return on assets compare with the best in the industry? Over the past few years, has it been improving or declining? What companies in any industry have the highest margins, the highest velocity, or the highest return on assets? What can you learn from them?

One truth about business is that the return on assets has to be greater than the cost of using your own and other people's (bankers' and shareholders') money, the *cost of capital*. If the return on assets does not exceed the cost of capital (which is typically 10 percent or more), there will be real discontent among the investors because management is destroying shareholder wealth.

Some companies have businesses, divisions, or product lines that do not earn the cost of capital. They therefore have to either improve the return or get rid of these lines of business. That's how many CEOs or business unit executives make the decision to sell (divest) a business or discontinue a product line. Jack Welch used this principle at GE in the early 1980s when he said that any business within GE that could not be number one or two in its industry and did not earn the appropriate return on shareholder investment had to be either fixed or sold.

Even if you don't know your company's cost of capital, you can make a difference by suggesting ways to improve the return. If, for example, you work for an automobile company, you might find that the return on small cars is problematic. Auto manufacturers around the world have in fact been earning less than 2 percent return on their automotive assets on small cars, which is less than the cost of capital. How might that part of the business generate a higher return? Think about both parts of return on assets: margin and velocity.

GROWTH

Growth is vital to prosperity. Every person, every company, and every national economy must grow. Are you working for a company that is growing? Is it growing profitably and with no decline in velocity? What happens when the growth rate is low or even negative?

If the company as a whole or your business unit lags behind competitors, your personal progress will suffer. If the company's sales are flat for five or six years, people will not have the opportunity to be promoted and move forward. Top managers will begin to cut costs, cut the number of employees, cut layers. They'll start reining in R&D and advertising, good people will leave, and eventually the company will go into a death spiral. People will suffer.

In today's world, no growth means lagging behind in a world that grows every day. If you don't grow, competitors will eventually overtake you. Westinghouse, for example, used to be compared with GE. It lost its way, didn't focus on growth and productivity, and no longer exists. Then there was Digital Equipment Corporation, not long ago the world's second-largest computer com-

If You've Heard of Shareholder Value . . .

Every business must earn a return that is greater than the cost of using other people's money (banks', shareholders', or owners'). To keep this truth front and center, many companies today are using a measure called *shareholder value added*. SVA is a kind of shorthand for judging how well the business is performing overall. Is it or is it not meeting the basic requirements of investors?

But while SVA is a useful single measure and reflects the quality of money making, it's not much help in understanding what's really happening inside the business. That's why good CEOs never lose sight of the basic measures of money making—cash generation, margin, velocity, return on assets, and growth. It is by focusing on these elements that the street vendor makes his adjustments and continues to make money. And it's the same for a large company. Digging deeper into the realities that underlie cash generation, margin, velocity, return on assets, and growth provides the clues about where to focus attention and what to change.

pany. It stuck with making mid-sized computers when the world was going to PCs. While upstart PC makers like Dell and Compaq grew, Digital Equipment did not. It lost its independence when Compaq acquired it.

Growth has a psychological dimension. Growth energizes a business. A company that is expanding attracts talented people with fresh ideas. It stretches them and creates new opportunities. People like to hear customers say they're the best and that more business will be coming their way.

Look at what is happening in the world of Internet and other technology companies. Until very recently, young people were so anxious to get jobs working for dot-com companies that they were postponing their formal education. And venerable old companies had trouble luring graduates from the best schools and retaining their top performers while companies like Cisco, Intel, Nokia, Microsoft, and Oracle attracted a disproportionate number of them. Even a small start-up like Teligent attracted the former president of AT&T, Alex Mandl. What is the attraction? Growth, and all the opportunities and excitement it brings. The chance to build something, make something happen, and prosper.

Growing the Right Way

But growth for its own sake doesn't do any good. Growth has to be profitable and sustainable. You want growth to be accompanied by improved margins and velocity, and the cash generation must be able to keep pace.

Many entrepreneurs taste success on a small scale and become obsessed with growth, losing sight of the money-making basics along the way. The case of one entrepreneur who supplied beverage equipment to restaurants is typical. He built a profitable business installing beverage equipment at a cost of $2,000 per installation and thereafter collecting $100 a month from the restaurant for the ingredients he supplied. He borrowed money to make the installations. The margin on the ingredients was so slim that it did not cover the interest payments on the borrowed money. Yet he was obsessed with growth.

As this ambitious young man expanded the business, the outflow of cash soon outpaced the flow of money into the business. Eventually, the company went bankrupt, and the lenders decided that the company needed a new CEO.

Sometimes senior management inadvertently encourages unprofitable growth by giving the sales force the wrong incentives. For example, one $16-million injection molding company rewarded its sales representatives based on how many dollars' worth of plastic caps they sold, regardless of whether the company made a profit on them. Everyone was excited when the company landed $4 million in new sales from two major customers. But in the following three years, as sales rose, profit margins shrank. Finally, the CEO realized that the new business everyone was so excited about was actually a money loser. The price of the new caps did not cover the costs of producing them. Worse, the sales team lowered the price each year to retain the business.

Bankruptcy is often the sad end of misguided expansion plans. In August 2000, one of the largest equipment retailers in the United States joined the list of companies seeking bankruptcy protection when its ambitious growth plans went awry.

In the 1990s, the company had kicked off a rapid expansion that included opening eighty to a hundred stores a year, some outside the United States for the first time ever. Sales grew steadily through the 1990s, from well under $500 million to well over $2 billion, and at least in the early years, earnings per share inched up, too. But beginning in 1995, as the pace of its acquisitions quickened, earnings moved sharply downward for several reasons.

For one thing, the company was conducting business much as it always had, trying to make money on the sale of the equipment itself and also on the highly lucrative business of extending credit to customers. Meanwhile, the credit card industry was blossoming, and customers were using credit cards instead of store credit to buy their equipment. The company lost a main source of income. The loans it did make were more often to high-risk customers, some of whom didn't make their payments. Also, sales from the new stores didn't always meet expectations, and sales from older stores were dwindling as the company failed to make needed renovations.

By 1998, the company was losing money, and in 1999, it began to retrench. It closed stores and sold off some of its business units. Still the debt burden was too great, and in August 2000, under the leadership of a newly appointed CEO, the company filed for Chapter 11 bankruptcy.

So don't use size as a measure of success. Pushing for more sales dollars isn't necessarily good business. You have to know how and why you're growing. And you have to consider whether you are growing in a way that can continue.

Look at what is happening to your cash. Maybe sales are increasing, but the cash situation is getting worse. Step back. Are you growing in a way that is generating or consuming cash? Is your profit margin improving or getting worse?

If the money making is improving and the cash is growing too, you have some interesting choices. You can use the funds to develop a new product, buy another company, or expand into a new country. Maybe you want to add some new features to make your product more appealing. Maybe you can cut the price and expand demand profitably.

Finding opportunities for profitable growth when others can't is part of business acumen. Sam Walton, the founder of Wal-Mart, knew how to grow a business, even when his industry peers thought it was impossible. In 1975, the CEO of Sears, Roebuck told my class at Northwestern University's Kellogg School of Business that retailing in the United States was a mature business and a no-growth industry. That's why he diversified into financial services. Meanwhile, Sam Walton was opening new stores while maintaining a return on assets substantially above the industry average.

Wal-Mart has widened the gap between itself and Sears. Though the businesses were roughly equal in size in 1992, Wal-Mart had sales of $165 billion for the year ending January 31, 2000, versus Sears's sales of roughly $40 billion for the same period. In the process of expanding, Wal-Mart's margin and velocity have both improved. Wal-Mart's superior return on assets provides resources for it to expand internationally.

Opportunities for profitable growth may not be obvious, especially for big, established companies. But with drive, tenacity and risk taking, you and your colleagues can discover them. Take, for example, Ford. As Jac Nasser told the investment community at a meeting with securities analysts in January 1999, Ford was evaluating several avenues of growth and would pursue those that had the greatest potential to create value. One of Ford's growth options was to provide a range of services that have to do with vehicle ownership. Nasser intended to have Ford venture down this path by making acquisitions and exploiting adjacencies. *Adjacencies* is the word he uses to describe market segments that are different from but closely related to the core business— like Nike's selling of athletic apparel along with its core business of selling athletic shoes.

As Ford saw it, a consumer who buys a vehicle needs to finance it, insure it, and, over time, maintain it and buy replacement parts. Financing, insurance, maintenance, and auto parts are separate market segments, but they are closely related to the initial vehicle purchase. Over the life of the car, an average person spends $68,000 in total—almost three and a half times what the average consumer pays for a vehicle. Ford hoped to grow and create shareholder value by participating in all these segments. That's why in 1999 it acquired Kwik-Fit, a European auto repair chain, and Automobile Protection Corporation, which provides extended service contracts on all makes of cars.

Ford also planned to fuel growth by using e-commerce aggressively. The company plans to use the Internet to connect with more customers more quickly and to communicate with suppliers and dealers to shorten the time it takes to provide consumers with the vehicles they desire. That way both customer satisfaction and sales would rise.

CUSTOMERS

The street vendor knows his customers well. Simply by watching them, he can detect whether they like his fruit

or are growing dissatisfied, and whether their prefer-
ences are changing. CEOs with business acumen have
the same close connection with customers and strong
conviction that the business cannot thrive without satis-
fying them. It's universal.

Although many companies use scientific research
methods like surveys and focus groups to try to understand consumer needs, the best CEOs don't rely on clin-
ical data alone. They know that if they become removed
from the action, they may miss important changes and
opportunities in the marketplace. Many of them make
special efforts to observe and talk directly with the people who use their products and services. Sam Walton is
the quintessential example of a CEO who never lost
touch with consumers. Even when he was running a
$30 billion retailing empire, he regularly visited stores
to see for himself how things were going.

Soon after Bob Nardelli arrived at The Home Depot
as the new CEO in 2000, he visited many stores across
the United States. He put on one of the orange aprons
The Home Depot is known for, mixed in with employees, and waited on customers. That way, he could see
for himself how customers and employees were inter-
acting and detect why shoppers returned repeatedly.
The close contact with customers gave him ideas for
taking the company to the next level by introducing
new product segments, for example, and freeing up
employees' time by having the stock replenished during
slow times.

Jac Nasser, too, spent time with consumers in various parts of the world to see and hear firsthand how

they use Ford cars and trucks. When he traveled to various countries, he made a point of visiting places where young people congregate to observe trends in color and style.

Direct contact provides insight other kinds of market research cannot. In one instance, when Nasser was visiting with a group of Hispanic youths in Miami, one of the drivers said he had not added any accessories to his car. But when Nasser got in the car to drive with the young man, he saw that the car did in fact have several new accessories, including a trailer hitch, a special wide-angle rearview mirror, rubber mats, and driving lamps. The owner didn't think to mention the items because they had become "so much a part of the car."

Nasser's belief about the importance of being close to consumers led to the decision to relocate Ford's Lincoln Mercury division to California, when Ford's share of luxury cars was shrinking in that market in the period 1997–1998. That way, the leaders of the luxury car group would have direct contact with the affluent California consumers who set the trends in the luxury car market.

The best CEOs know that focusing solely on money making at the expense of customers is shortsighted. That's why Jac Nasser responded as he did to the recall of 6.5 million Firestone tires used on Ford Explorers in August 2000. Nasser idled three plants for three weeks to speed availability of replacement tires. He realized that while Ford's money making would suffer temporarily, customer safety had to come first. After all, without customers' trust, the rest doesn't matter.

At your company, you may talk about the people who buy and use your products as "customers." They may or may not be the people who ultimately use the product—the consumers. It's important to understand both. When Colgate-Palmolive develops new products, it tries to understand the needs and wants of the *consumer,* but many of its processes—logistics, discounts, order scheduling, shelving, merchandising—are geared to serve *customers* like Wal-Mart.

As you think about consumers, keep it simple. How can you describe what consumers are buying? It might not be the physical product alone. Maybe they're buying reliability, convenience, or service. For many businesses and for the street vendor, what consumers are buying includes trustworthiness.

Many businesses run into trouble because the leaders lose touch with consumers. Let's use Sears again as an example of how important it is to know consumers. In the late 1980s and early 1990s, middle-class women were buying clothing from up-scale department stores, which were cutting prices of high-margin name-brand apparel, or from discounters, which were upgrading their clothing while keeping prices low. Sears missed the trend completely. It was buying clothing from the same suppliers it had used for years, at prices that were not competitive with the discounters'. Consumers were getting neither the styles nor the prices they wanted.

Arthur Martinez, who joined Sears in 1992 to run the merchandise division and became CEO in 1995, picked up on the fact that women consumers simply didn't like the clothing Sears was offering. Sears expanded and redesigned the women's clothing departments, which were generating almost two-thirds of operating income (profits from the normal operations of the business, not adjusted for income and expenses from selling assets, paying federal taxes, and the like). It began to emphasize popular name brands and advertised the changes through its "softer side of Sears" campaign.

Sears's focus on the consumer paid off: Sales rose steadily from $29 billion in 1994 to $31 billion in 1995 and $33 billion in 1996. Operating income rose, too, from 4.9 percent of sales, to 5.4 percent, to 6.1 percent in those same years. (In the late 1990s, Sears again lost its footing under intense competition from Target, Wal-Mart, and other retailers.)

When you can't get the prices and margins you used to get, talk to consumers to understand why. Observe them directly, unfiltered, not through the eyes of distributors or other middlemen.

Some people talk about customer loyalty. But you have to earn loyalty every time you come in contact with the customer. Customers need a simple reason to buy from you. You have to give them something they really need or want. You can find out what they need— from them. It's common sense. You would be surprised how often this common sense of business is lacking.

3

Understanding Your Company's Total Business

HOW THE PIECES COME TOGETHER

The elements of money making—cash generation, margin, velocity, return on assets, and growth—can all be measured. But people with business acumen don't just memorize these words like terms in a textbook. They understand their real meaning, instinctively sense their relationships to one another, and use them to create a mental picture. True businesspeople combine the elements of money making to get an intuitive grasp of the total business.

A doctor's diagnosis is a simple comparison. A doctor takes your pulse, blood count, temperature, and so on. From simple measurements, she can deduce what is happening with your body. Nevertheless, regardless of how many tests have been conducted, a good diagnosis requires judgment of the body's overall health. Is it improving or declining? A good doctor can even save your life by deducing that the body is being affected by an untreated disease.

When Jack Welch announced a 21 percent increase in GE's second-quarter earnings in July 2000, he was quoted in the press release as saying that the result showed the company's ability to deliver "top-line growth, increased margins and strong cash generation." You can see the business thinking—cash, margin, and growth. GE's operating margin was up from the year before, sales had risen, and the company had generated $5.9 billion in cash in the first half of the year. The fundamentals indicated that GE was doing well as a total business.

Welch has mastered the relationships between cash generation, margin, velocity, return on assets, growth, and customers. He knows that if a company continuously improves productivity, then margins improve and cash is generated. When margins and velocity improve, you have the leeway to take better care of customers, thus you can get a larger share of the market and the company grows.

Let's use another illustration drawn from Ford Motor Company archives and *The Public Image of Henry Ford* by David L. Lewis. Henry Ford had an intuitive sense of how the total business made money. He not only made legendary breakthroughs in manufacturing techniques but also reduced the price of a touring car every year from 1909 to 1915 and introduced the $5 workday.

Henry Ford seemed to understand that lower prices and higher wages had a relationship to each other that contributed to money making. In 1914, Ford announced that the company would pay workers a minimum of $5 a day. The wage hike was huge—up from $2.34—and came during a mild worldwide depression and at a time when other automobile companies were paying their workers less than half that much.

Higher wages gave more people the wherewithal to buy a car. A French scholar summed it up, writing in the 1950s that the $5 day "made every worker a potential customer." More customers meant more money, therefore more freedom to lower prices. Lower prices made cars affordable by even more people, and so on.

Another story further illustrates Henry Ford's business acumen. In 1916, the Dodge brothers, who owned a stake in Ford, filed a lawsuit because they wanted higher dividends. During the court case, their attorney challenged Henry Ford's approach to running the business.

The attorney questioned how the owners could benefit if Mr. Ford continued to "employ a great army of men at high wages, to reduce the selling price of your car, so that a lot of people can buy it at a cheap price, and give everybody a car that wants one."

Mr. Ford was quite taken by this characterization of his business approach. He replied: "If you give all that, the money will fall into your hands; you can't get out of it." Henry Ford knew that Ford Motor Company had a winning formula. The elements of money making—cash generation, margin, velocity, return, growth, and customers—and the relationships between them created a robust business that could continue to make money.

Henry Ford had fun making money. That same sense of fun and excitement can be yours if you start applying the universal law of business to your company. But first you have to gather some basic information.

Begin with the basics of money making. Then try to get a feel for how they work together. Look at your company through the eyes of a street vendor. You probably know a lot about the history of the company—the kinds of products or services it sells, and how many manufacturing facilities it has, for example. They tend to be common knowledge at most companies. A street vendor knows similar things—his suppliers, for example, the people who supply the fruit he sells.

But now the difference between the street vendor and most people in business emerges. See if you can answer the following questions for your company. We'll show you the answers for two companies, Ford Automotive (the part of Ford Motor Company that sells cars and trucks) and Gateway Computer:

- *What were your company's sales during the last year?*
    For Ford Automotive, they were $137.0 billion worldwide in 1999, an all-time high.

    For Gateway, they were $8.6 billion in 1999, the highest ever, and $1.2 billion more than the previous year.
- *Is the company growing? Or is growth flat or declining? Is this growth picture good enough?*
    Ford's sales were up 15 percent from 1998 to 1999. They had dropped 3 percent from 1997 to 1998. Before that, sales had been growing by 5 percent annually, in part because the product mix included more higher-priced vehicles.

Gateway's sales have been rising steadily for the past decade. From 1998 to 1999, sales increased 15.7 percent.

- *What is your company's profit margin? Is it growing, declining, or flat?*

Ford Automotive's margin, after taxes, was 4.2 percent in 1999. That's the best it's been since 1988.

Gateway's margin, after taxes, was 4.9 percent, slightly better than the 4.6 percent of the year before. (Does 4 percent remind you of anything—say, a Wal-Mart or a grocery store? It should. At its core, a PC company is not much different from a grocery store. Both businesses are extremely competitive and sell goods that can quickly become obsolete.)

- *How does your margin compare with your competitors'? How does it compare with those of other industries?*

Ford's margin was higher than GM's and also higher than Toyota's for the year ending 1999.

Gateway's margin was higher than Compaq's (1.5 percent) but lower than Dell's (7.4 percent).

- *Do you know your company's inventory velocity? its asset velocity?*

Ford's inventory velocity was about 21, but that does *not* include vehicles in transit between the plant and the dealer or on the dealer's lot. Combining all these factors would greatly reduce its inventory velocity. Ford's asset velocity is very different from its inventory velocity. When you consider Ford's investment in manufacturing plants, buildings, equipment, tools, and accounts receivable, in addition to its investment in inventories, the velocity changes from 21 to 1.3 for the year ended 1999. Ford's asset velocity is 1.3.

Gateway's inventory velocity was a healthy 45. Its asset velocity—sales divided by total assets, not just by inventory—was 12.6.

• *What is your company's return on assets?*

If you know the margin and the velocity, you can figure it out using $R = M \times V$. Here's how it works for Ford:

$$R = M \times V$$

Ford's return on assets = 4.2 percent after-tax margin × 1.3 asset velocity

For Ford, the R is about 5.5 percent, not up to the aspirations of management. Now let's do the thinking for Gateway, again using $R = M \times V$:

$$R = M \times V$$

Gateway's return on assets = 4.9 percent after-tax margin × 12.6 asset velocity

Gateway's return on assets is 61.7 percent. Shareholders should like that.

• *Is your company's cash generation increasing or decreasing? Why is it going one way or the other?*

Ford had $23.6 billion in cash at the end of 1999—about the same amount it had at the end of 1998. But Ford bought Volvo and made some other investments for growth. How did Ford generate cash? The company scrutinized major investments in fixed assets and worked to reduce inventory. Ford was a net cash generator.

Gateway generated $731 million in cash from operations in 1999, a little less than in 1998. It, too, was a net cash generator.

- *Is your company gaining or losing against the competition?*

In 1999, Ford was maintaining strong market share in North America.

Gateway's market share had been increasing and was very strong among consumers (versus business customers). Dell and Compaq continued to dominate the overall PC market, and IBM's share was eroding.

If you can answer these questions for your company, you are speaking the universal language of business. You're getting a picture of your company's *total business,* the kind a shopkeeper would have. And it doesn't take a lot of numbers to get there—sales, margin, total inventories, assets, and cash. You can pull these numbers out of the annual report. And you don't need pinpoint accuracy to understand the reality of the company.

Let's recap the fundamentals of Ford in 1999:

- Sales of $137.0 billion in 1999; sales up from 1998 to 1999, but down from 1997 to 1998.
- Maintaining strong market share in major markets.
- Margin of 4.2 percent after taxes.
- Asset velocity of 1.3.
- Very low inventory velocity (including vehicles in transit and on dealers' lots).
- Generating cash.

Now let's recap Gateway Computer:

- Sales of $8.6 billion in 1999; sales up over 1998.
- Market share on the rise.
- Margin of 4.9 percent after taxes.
- Asset velocity of 12.6.
- Very high inventory velocity of 45.
- Generating cash.

Suppose you worked for Ford in 1999 and you knew that the company was a net cash generator, that its margins were very good compared with its competitors' but low compared with those of other industries, that sales growth was not as good as you would like and velocity was low, what would you do? Would you have a better sense of what to focus on? Would you have a sense of urgency? You might look for ways to improve customer satisfaction or increase productivity. You might focus on developing exciting new products and work hard to launch them quickly. And you might make extra efforts to ensure that big investments are made in areas where the business is growing profitably.

Now let's say you worked for Gateway. Gateway's margin isn't much better than Ford's, but its inventory velocity is fantastic. Its return on assets is great. The company is growing and improving market share, but its market share is still small compared with those of Dell and Compaq. Increased market share would be a tremendous help in competing against the two giants. Would you look for ways to improve market share through new products and services? Would a picture of the total business focus your attention?

We have provided the questions to help you understand your company. Ask your investor relations department for the information you need to answer them. The numbers are also available now on most companies' Web sites. Security analysts at firms like Merrill Lynch also have this information. For public companies, you can get it from the annual report, available directly online from the U.S. Securities and Exchange Commission (www.sec.gov/edaux/searches.htm).

Let there be no doubt—none of this information is confidential. Your asking for it will demonstrate to management your keen desire to think beyond the silos and help the total business.

In my work with most private companies (those without shareholders), management is often willing to share the information but believes people don't understand it or are not interested. Bring your desire to their attention. They are likely to react positively. Maybe this book will encourage them to disperse it regularly.

Maybe you can persuade your bosses that the universal language of business does not belong in the executive suite alone. Cash generation, margin, velocity, return on assets, growth, and customers should be part of everyone's vocabulary. Remind them that employees can contribute more when they know what really goes on in the business and can apply their business acumen.

Part II

BUSINESS ACUMEN IN THE REAL WORLD

4

The World Has Complexity, Leaders Provide Clarity

FIGURING OUT BUSINESS PRIORITIES

You now know something about the real world of a street vendor and a CEO and how they are similar. The street vendor uses his business acumen to gauge the outside environment and make decisions on prices, margins, and purchasing. You have a sense of what it's like to make trade-offs between reducing prices, thereby selling more and generating cash, and not reducing prices, which might mean keeping inventory for the next day and running the risk of perished fruit or unhappy customers.

Let's now look at the real world of companies, small, medium, or large, many of which are publicly traded and are punished heavily by the stock market for missing a commitment by as little as a penny per share of stock. What the CEOs of these companies know—that most of us don't—is how to use the same common sense that street vendors use to perceive what's really changing in the outside world and to cut through the complexity of their businesses. They use their business acumen to determine clear, specific priorities, or action items, that make money in the real world and create wealth for stockholders or owners.

Every business has some degree of complexity. Take Ford, in 1999, the second-largest automotive concern in the world. It had about 350,000 employees, sold about 7 million vehicles each year (that's 20,000 a day) in 200 countries and territories, and operated 112 plants in 38 countries, each of which had its own economic picture, currency, consumer trends, competitive dynamics, and social concerns. Ford had eight primary vehicle brands (Ford, Lincoln, Mercury, Volvo, Jaguar, Aston Martin, Land Rover, and Mazda, the last of which was 33 percent owned by Ford) as well as numerous nameplate brands (Mustang, Focus, and so on) with various options on each vehicle. Ford had dozens of competitors worldwide—not just other car manufacturers but also major banks and credit unions, which compete with Ford Credit, the world's largest automotive financing company. Overlay on this complexity another two considerations that are totally uncontrollable and unpredictable: currency fluctuations (for example, the value of the euro—the monetary unit of countries in the European Union—moved 25 percent against the dollar in 1999–2000) and persistent uncertainty about interest rates set by the Fed (higher interest rates will eventually slow the economy and reduce demand for cars and trucks).

Exceptional business leaders do what no computer can do. They scan the external environment, and out of all the things that are going on in the world, they are able to identify the significant patterns and trends.

It's not pure guesswork to predict that a new market will be created or a new need generated. After all, the future is created from what already exists. The key technologies necessary for the PC—the monitor, the disk drives, the mouse, the keyboards, the micro-processors, the software, and the laser printers—all existed in the mid-1970s. The seeds had been planted, yet Apple caught the office-automation giants off guard. Xerox advertised its PC, the Alto, on television in 1979, in the first-ever PC commercial. IBM introduced its first PC in 1981.

But meanwhile, Steve Jobs, working with Steve Wozniak, had the business acumen to see the money-making potential of a machine that promised indepen-dence and freedom. Working in a garage, they got Apple off the ground in 1976. No venture capitalists were needed. Apple made money in its first month and hit a billion dollars in sales within ten years.

The best CEOs use their business acumen to reduce complexity, whether internal or external to the com-pany, to the basics of money making. They relish the mental challenge. Doing so helps them discover any flaws in their logic and gives them confidence that they are on the right path. It helps them make the right trade-offs and makes them more decisive.

Business acumen helps a CEO choose the three or four business priorities (no more than five) that will retain customers and achieve all the important money-making goals at the same time—all in the context of the real world.

A business priority defines the most important action that needs to be taken at a certain point in time. At GE today, e-commerce—doing business on the Internet—is a business priority. Here's why. Jack Welch, always willing to learn from anyone, anywhere, anytime, was quick to recognize that the Internet could improve the cost, speed, and quality of transactions involved in the transfer of money and information between GE and its suppliers and alliance partners. A transaction that once cost $1 could cost as little as $2\frac{1}{2}$ cents on-line and be completed much faster. Costs would go down, and productivity would improve; hence margins would increase. Fewer assets would be involved in the transaction process, so velocity would improve. And if GE acted before competitors, it could gain an edge in the market and feed its growth.

Or look at Ford's business priorities. In 1997, Jac Nasser, at the time in charge of worldwide Ford Automotive Operations, came to the conclusion that an environment of declining prices would continue. He made a bold judgment and announced to the world that he did not believe a general price increase was sustainable. He would make money in the business without an overall price increase by focusing on the right priorities. Margins could not decline, he said, and growth was still an imperative.

The two business priorities Nasser set were, first, cost reductions of $1 billion each year with appropriate programs and follow-through, and second, capital investment reduction of $1 billion. Some products and even nameplate brands that required additional capital expenditures, such as the Aerostar and the previous Cougar, had to be eliminated. The judgment and business priorities proved correct. Ford delivered superior margin, cash generation, return on assets, and growth with stable pricing.

The world then changed. By 2000, with cost reduction a way of life at Ford, the business priorities shifted to customer satisfaction and e-commerce. These priorities guided not just Ford's day-to-day business decisions but also its response to the unexpected, whether a crisis or an opportunity. Ford's focus on e-commerce, for example, led to the timely formation of Covisint, an on-line purchasing exchange, with GM and other auto manufacturers.

Ford's emphasis on customer satisfaction helped the CEO act decisively during the Firestone tire recall. It became the central criterion in deciding how to respond and led to the decision to temporarily suspend production of new vehicles at several plants so that customers would have replacement tires sooner. It also set the tone for communications inside and outside the company during the crisis.

In mid 2000, Kmart, the granddaddy of discounters that ceded its number one status to Wal-Mart in the 1990s, set out to improve its velocity and margin and create a positive experience for customers. In September 2000, the senior team, led by new CEO Chuck Conaway, established several business priorities, including improving the logistics of the business. The company had to buy the right merchandise at the right price, get it on the shelves as quickly and as efficiently as possible, and draw customers in by creating a pleasant ambiance. By mid 2001, investors were growing skeptical that the company would act on the priorities. The focus, though, was clear and linked to the fundamentals of the business.

FROM COMPLEXITY TO SIMPLICITY

Use your business acumen and think about the business challenge as a brain teaser. There are internal things and external things to consider, all of which can vary. For each variable, anything from interest rates to market trends and government regulation, there's the present status as well as projections about the future. Look at the big picture and see how the variables might come together. Then consider the business fundamentals. How might the fundamentals of money making work together given your ideas about patterns and trends? What are the relationships between them? How will meeting the business priorities turn the company into a money-making machine?

Low inventory is a priority at Dell Computer, for several money-making reasons. Dell's low inventory means the company does not have to use its cash to buy components and make products that sit on the shelf for weeks or months. Also, in the PC business, product obsolescence is a huge risk, and prices of parts are continually falling. If your inventory is very current, you have less risk that customers will reject products because they are not the latest technology. And if component prices decline each week, you can take advantage of the reductions. You can cut prices to the consumer, thereby making your product more appealing, while preserving your already slim margin. Michael Dell has the business acumen to see the logical connections between these things and understand the importance of managing inventory.

Look at another example of how Jack Welch applied business acumen to make the right business decisions. Just after Ronald Reagan retired from the presidency in January of 1989, external changes caused Welch to reevaluate GE's aerospace business. With the cold war ending, the old Soviet Union disintegrating, and the Berlin Wall being torn down, it was clear that the U.S. defense budget would decline and the defense industry itself would begin to shrink.

GE could have become a bigger player in that arena through the merger and acquisition activity that was sure to follow. But focusing on the fundamentals, Welch concluded that growth, return on assets, and cash generation would not meet investors' criteria. A better course of action was to sell the business to the company he believed would emerge as the dominant player: Martin Marietta. He indeed sold GE's aerospace business to Martin Marietta for a combination of cash and stock. Through continued mergers, Martin Marietta then became Lockheed Martin, the largest defense contractor in the world. GE sold its stock in Lockheed Martin after a substantial run-up in the price. Thus Welch created tremendous value for GE shareholders by recognizing changes in the outside world and using the fundamentals of business to guide his decisions.

Even if you're not a CEO, business acumen can help you cut through the complexity to make the right decisions every day. Say you're a marketing manager in a consumer goods company. You manage four product lines—laundry soaps, dish detergents, toothpaste, and household cleansers. Do you really know which product lines make money? which one makes the most money? which one makes the least? Do you know which ones consume cash? which ones generate it? Is one product line more volatile than the others? You should know these things, just as the street vendor knows his apples from his oranges.

Maybe you're an engineer designing a new product. How does it fit into the company's total money-making picture? Will the design please customers *and* earn a good margin? Does it have the features lots of customers want? Is it preferred by customers over that of a competitor? Is it going to require new equipment and thus consume cash and reduce velocity? Or is it simply an extension of some existing products and therefore uses equipment or tooling the company already has?

If your design uses existing equipment, it conserves cash. If you get more sales using the same assets, velocity will increase. You as an engineer can make a contribution by thinking this way—exercising your business acumen. Ford is one company that has trained its engineers to use this kind of business thinking.

Maybe you're in sales. You generate a lot of business by selling to large customers. But they negotiate hard. They want big discounts and they want long credit terms—90 days instead of the usual 45. Try using your business acumen to figure out how to create value for the customer without having to give more than the usual credit terms and discounts. If, for example, you are selling to a company like Wal-Mart, maybe you can find a way to increase the velocity of your products on their shelf. That way Wal-Mart benefits without additional discounts. This is the business acumen of a street vendor.

Chances are you will face more complexity and volatility as you take on more responsibility in your job. Practice business acumen along the way so you will have the courage to face complexity. Many business leaders falter because they become overwhelmed or indecisive. Some do not set clear priorities, or they lose focus, especially if their judgments come into question. If the leader fails to set priorities, keeps changing his mind, or communicates them poorly, the whole organization loses energy.

If, on the other hand, he sets business priorities and communicates them clearly and often, people will have a better sense of what to do. If he chooses the "right" set of business priorities, the business can flourish.

In some cases, CEOs succeed for a while because they can engineer mergers and acquisitions and weave persuasive stories for security analysts on Wall Street. They're known as deal makers. But without business acumen, they don't last long. Once deals get done, the business needs something else, something they cannot provide: focus on the basics of the business. More than once I've heard directors say things like, "Sure, she understands Wall Street, but can she really run the business?" or "Is he a businessman or is he just a deal maker?"

The CEO of a U.S.–based multinational company is a case in point. Wall Street praised the man highly for engineering the purchase of a European competitor. The two companies had complementary strengths and would be a real powerhouse in the global industry. Investors were pleased—but not for long. Soon after the companies were merged, investors began to discover that deal making is one thing, business acumen is quite another. The CEO did not set clear business priorities for the new company, so redundant activities and functions did not get eliminated quickly enough, and the two former companies were not coordinating their marketing efforts. The merger was good, but the hoped-for benefits—better profitability and growth—were not materializing. The board had to ask the CEO to resign. This scenario has been repeated many times.

5

Wealth Is More Than Making Money

SEEING THE BUSINESS LIKE AN INVESTOR

The main task for the CEO of a publicly traded company goes beyond money making. Shareholders (and employees who receive stock options as part of their compensation) expect a CEO to create wealth for them. The best CEOs understand that money making and wealth creation are linked through what is known as the *price-earnings multiple*—also called the *P-E multiple,* or *P-E ratio.* The P is the price of an individual share of stock. The E is earnings per share—how much profit the company made for each share of stock.

Yes, the P-E multiple is a number (P divided by E), but don't get lost in the calculation. You can get the exact number for your company from people in your finance department or from the stock price listings in the *Wall Street Journal.*

A P-E multiple of, say, 7 means that for every dollar of earnings per share, the stock is worth seven times that much. Obviously, the higher the P-E multiple, the more wealth is created.

Basically, the P-E multiple represents expectations about a company's current and future money-making ability. It reflects the quality of the money-making formula—the combination of expected cash generation, margin, velocity, return on assets, and profitable revenue growth—vis-à-vis the competition and in the future. But the P-E multiple is not pure speculation. Most often, it is based on a track record and on investors' confidence that management will be able to sustain the money-making formula.

P-E multiples vary from industry to industry and company to company, and they can change over time. P-E multiples have been known to plummet when companies miss their money-making goals. Any inconsistency calls into question the predictability of cash generation, margin, velocity, return on assets, and growth. (Investors hate inconsistency and volatility.) On the other hand, P-E multiples can be enhanced by delivering on money-making commitments consistently and predictably over time. (Investors love consistency and predictability quarter by quarter.)

Let's take an example of what drives the P-E multiple. Compare Coca-Cola and Pepsi. Coca-Cola's multiple has been consistently higher than arch rival Pepsi's for more than fifteen years. Managers of both companies work hard. They're ambitious and aggressive. But for the past fifteen years, Coca-Cola's P-E multiple has been, on average, 4 points higher than Pepsi's. Shareholders have valued the stock of Coca-Cola higher than that of Pepsi. This is because shareholders have anticipated that

Coke's combination of cash generation, margins, velocity, return on assets, and profitable revenue growth would be better than Pepsi's. More recently, Coke has had some setbacks and a change of leadership while Pepsi has been trying to find new areas for growth. It remains to be seen whether investors will continue to expect Coke to do better than Pepsi, as it has for more than a decade.

Even if your company is privately held, the same principles apply. Public scrutiny creates good discipline, but private companies can create their own discipline. Doing the right things day in and day out builds value. Remember, private companies often get sold or go public, and their value is determined by the same principles that underlie the P-E multiple.

WHERE THE P-E MULTIPLE COMES FROM

Market forces really determine a company's P-E multiple, based on the assessments of individual investors and security analysts. Security analysts have the job of deciding what they think is an appropriate P-E multiple for the companies they track. If their assessment shows that the company deserves a higher P-E multiple than the market reflects, their firms tend to buy the company's stock. The opposite is also true: If the market reflects a higher P-E multiple than the security analysts think the company deserves, they tend to sell its stock.

It's not at all unusual for two security analysts to have contradictory recommendations, because their recommendations involve some degree of judgment. But security analysts do use certain guidelines and make certain comparisons. They typically look at the company compared with other companies in its industry, and they compare the industry to the total market. Thus the P-E multiple and the price of the stock evolve as security analysts and investors around the world make such determinations and recommendations about the company's stock.

A common comparison is to look at the P-E multiple of an individual company against the average P-E multiple of the Standard & Poor's 500—a collection of five hundred companies that are widely held and represent the broad economy of the nation. Comparisons against averages, or *indexes,* of a range of companies are telling. For instance, while the average P-E multiple of the S&P 500 during the summer of 2000 was 23, the P-E ratio of the American auto industry averaged around 8. That tells you that investors did not value the automotive industry's future performance as highly as they valued that of many other companies and that of the S&P 500 companies combined. To put it more bluntly, investors discounted the value of two of the world's largest companies, Ford and GM, by 65 percent compared with the S&P 500 (8 is roughly 35 percent of 23, so the stock prices of Ford and GM were discounted by 65 percent compared with the S&P 500 average).

The major reason for such a deep discount is that in the past, the auto industry has shown deeply disappointing performance whenever the economy went into recession. Most security analysts still see the American auto industry as a cyclical industry that is prone to deliver very poor results as money gets tight or interest rates increase sharply. Cyclical industries lack the consistency and predictability investors like, and therefore generally have lower P-E multiples than noncyclical industries.

P-E multiples can also vary widely within an industry. In retailing, for example, in August 2000, Wal-Mart's P-E multiple was 35, while Sears was in the single digits.

Maybe you're wondering how dot-com companies fit in. Internet companies are a recent phenomenon that investors were learning how to deal with. There was no set of commonly understood guidelines in valuing these companies, many of which had no earnings. Investors and security analysts actually put the old guidelines aside. Initially, these dot-com stocks were trading at a multiple of their revenues, not of their earnings, since few of them ever made any money. Strictly speaking, the term *P-E multiple* doesn't really fit.

The multiples of dot-com companies were based on some ten-year conjectures about how fast the companies could grow. The assumption was that if a company could be in the Internet space before anyone else, it could eventually (no one really knew when) dominate its market and dictate the profitability of its industry.

For many, that was a dream. Beginning in late 1999, we saw these extremely high valuations of dot-coms come crashing down the moment people began to challenge the premise that high-speed growth would eventually lead to huge profitability. These dot-com companies are huge cash guzzlers. They have what is known in Silicon Valley as a high burn rate. That is, because start-up companies have to buy equipment and pay salaries and marketing costs to develop interest in their product, they usually spend more cash per month than they take in from sales. However, for all businesses, cash is the blood supply. Without it, the dot-com companies must either be sold or go out of business altogether.

The world of Internet companies has evolved. Watch what's happened to the P-E multiple. And keep a tight hand on your hard-earned money!

MANAGING THE P-E MULTIPLE

A higher P-E multiple creates more shareholder wealth. A CEO with business acumen understands that. This truth puts even more importance on the money-making formula. If the formula is right, the company will make money. If the formula is right and the company executes it consistently over time, the P-E multiple will rise. The creation of wealth is even more dramatic because both the earnings and the multiple rise.

How you run the business affects the P-E multiple. Let's go back to Coke and Pepsi. For about ten years in a row, Pepsi's sales grew 14 percent every year, while Coke's sales grew just 10 percent a year. But Coke made a bigger profit on its sales, and its return on investment was consistently higher. Sure, Pepsi was growing in terms of total sales, but Coke was doing a better job of meeting the various money-making goals. Its growth was more profitable than Pepsi's. Investors noticed. Although Pepsi's P-E ratio rose a respectable 12 points (from 17 to 29) between 1990 and 1999, Coke's rose even more—27 points (from 20 to 47).

A publicly held company that grows the top line

(sales, or revenues) and the bottom line (profit, or earnings) consistently over time without lowering velocity will increase the P-E multiple. If you increase velocity, that's even better. The value of the stock rises, and shareholders become wealthier.

What happens if the company begins to miss the earnings-per-share expectations, even by a penny? The punishment can be extreme. In 2000, the stock prices of several companies tumbled as much as 25 to 40 percent or more in one day. It happened to Honeywell, Nordstrom, and Computer Associates. When, for example, in July 2000, Honeywell warned investors that earnings per share for the quarter might be anywhere from 1 to 5 cents lower than the projected 78 cents, the stock price fell 18 percent in one day and 10 percent the next. GE tried to buy company at what some called a bargain price.

When a company misses expectations, investors begin to question the company's discipline. Doubts arise about whether the company can deliver on its commitments going forward. And it's not just the stock price that falls. The P-E multiple declines, too. So missing an earnings-per-share commitment by a penny or saying growth won't be as high as expected dramatically shrinks wealth creation. In the first half of 2000, Honeywell's P-E multiple fell significantly.

Such abrupt changes in valuations have dramatic repercussions. Try to picture what happens behind the scenes in such situations. Major investors, namely fund managers at firms such as Fidelity, Vanguard, and CalPERS that invest trillions of dollars, call the CEO, the

CFO (chief financial officer), the investor relations person, and board members incessantly. These investors don't necessarily delve into the details of how the company works. They track the money making. They begin to panic when one of their investments misses the expected money-making target more than two times in a year.

The CEO then spends his or her time reassuring investors that everything is okay. Energy is spent calming nerves instead of running the business. When Honeywell's stock price began to sink, CEO Michael Bonsignore was quoted in the *Wall Street Journal* in June 2000 as saying "This is all about building back our credibility."

But it's not a problem for the CEO alone. If the P-E multiple is depressed, the whole company is vulnerable. For one thing, its ability to buy other companies is significantly hampered. Instead of being the company that grows, it starts to become an acquisition target for other companies that want to grow.

Investment bankers have a product line, just like any industry. Theirs is known as mergers and acquisitions. A company might start showing up on an investment banker's radar screen of *underperforming companies.* Another company might be convinced that this company would be a bargain to buy. It can now afford to buy the entire business and will take on the task of improving its performance.

Here's an example. In the mid-1990s, AMP, Inc., the world's largest and most respected manufacturer of wire connectors, seemed poised for continued success. The company dominated its industry and sold products used in several growth industries, including telecommunications and computers. But AMP lost sight of the money-making fundamentals and allowed its margins, growth, and velocity to decline compared with those of its competitors. As a result, its multiple declined, and by 1998 the company became a takeover target, first by AlliedSignal and then, successfully, by Tyco. Tyco paid more than double the price of AMP's stock and set out to fix the underlying problems. It took only a year to make $1 billion in cost reductions, improve the margins and velocity, and get the acquired company back on a growth trajectory. Tyco's P-E and stock price both went up as a result of that acquisition.

We all know what happens when mergers and acquisitions take place. The financial logic is quite compelling. Most of the time it's based on *synergies,* meaning that the merged company can combine or eliminate such things as duplicate distribution facilities, sales forces, and accounting departments. The implementation of synergies usually boils down to cost reduction, and cost reduction affects everyone personally, at least for a while. The human cost is very high. It's fun to be a consolidator. It's misery to be a "consolidatee."

Find out what your company's P-E multiple is and how the multiple compares to that of its peers and the S&P 500. Then take a minute to reflect: Have you and your company been focused on consistent, predictable, profitable growth; sustainable sources of cash generation; improved margin and/or velocity; and thus return on assets, quarter by quarter? Are all of these combined better than your competitors', and are they improving against that of the S&P 500? If so, you don't have to be on the defensive. You may be on the offensive, looking for acquisitions in a consolidating industry. Chances are you're retaining your star performers and attracting other good people. It feels good to be part of such a thriving business.

Or is your company chronically underperforming and inconsistent in terms of the basics of money making? Is your company's P-E multiple therefore beginning to decline relative to those of competitors and of the S&P 500? Are your bosses and coworkers panicking, or are they avoiding reality?

Maybe your multiple is pretty high compared with your competitors' but pretty low compared with those of companies outside your industry. Take it as a sign that people think your industry has little room for growth. Then challenge that no-growth assumption. Remember, Wal-Mart created great market value in so-called low-growth markets. Ask your management lots of questions, and be prepared to help find the answers.

GE'S TRACK RECORD

Let's restate the link between making money and creating wealth. The best CEOs use their business acumen to cut through the complexity of their business, their industry, and the broader business environment. They continually improve the fundamentals of money making, and by doing so consistently and relentlessly over time, they create a track record. The investment community tends to reward such CEOs and companies with a higher P-E multiple, which creates tremendous wealth for shareholders. It creates job security and growth opportunities for employees, and wealth for those who receive stock options.

GE is perhaps the best example in the world of a company whose track record of money making boosted its P-E multiple and created wealth for shareholders. Let me remind you that in 1981, when Jack Welch became CEO of GE, Westinghouse and GE were running neck and neck. Westinghouse has since disappeared, and GE is now among the most valuable companies in the world. That is, if you took all the GE shares and multiplied them by the stock price, you would find that the company was worth nearly $500 billion in mid-2000. (Compare that with its market value of just $12 billion in 1981, when Jack Welch became CEO.) In 1995, GE's P-E multiple ranged from a low of 13 to a high of 19. Then in November 2000 it was 43—substantially higher than that of most companies of any significant size.

GE is huge and complex, and faces all the idiosyncracies of the world economy—volatility of currencies, interest rates, and so on. But it has relentlessly and consistently focused on the fundamentals of money making.

Look at what GE has been doing. It has delivered solid growth—sales growth of at least 6 percent a year (11 percent in 1999), operating margin improvement every year for seventeen years, earnings-per-share growth of 12 to 15 percent—quarter by quarter, for seventeen years in a row. GE's inventory velocity went from 5.8 in 1995 to about 10 in 1999. And GE generates cash, which it uses to buy back its own stock every year.

GE consistently delivers results and has realistic programs in place to continue to do so in the future. When investors see that consistency over many years, they begin to think it will continue. Investors are confident that GE has figured out a way to make consistently more money quarter after quarter, year after year. GE is a money machine.

All GE employees know that if they can't contribute to the money making, GE is not the place for them to work. So understanding cash generation, return on assets, and growth, and all the while anticipating and meeting customers' needs—in short, business acumen— is in the genes of the people who stay and thrive at the company. And GE is a leader in ensuring that GE employees share in the wealth they help create. GE employees at many levels, including secretaries, who have received stock options over the course of twenty-five years of normal service have become multimillionaires.

FORD'S EFFORTS TO BOOST ITS P-E MULTIPLE

Now let's look at Ford, a company that actively tried to improve its P-E multiple. In 1999, Ford's P-E multiple was a mere 8 compared with the S&P 500's average P-E multiple of 23. That's a huge gap, which CEO Jac Nasser tried to close, again, by using business acumen.

Every week Nasser wrote a one- to two-page letter to employees giving his candid thoughts on a business topic. The letter was sent by e-mail to all 350,000 Ford employees worldwide. When, in early 2000, Ford's stock price and P-E multiple steeply declined, Nasser's letter explained why. He then mapped out the business priorities that he believed would improve the P-E multiple.

One of the highest priorities was customer satisfaction. The reasoning went like this: It is the customer who pays the bills for every company. Improved satisfaction improves both velocity and margin, because your products won't sit around for long and customers will be willing to pay a little more for the qualities associated with your brand. Also, building relationships with, and therefore retaining, customers costs less than having to continually attract new ones. Customer satisfaction, therefore, will accelerate sales and earnings growth.

Another priority at Ford was the use of a tool known as *consumer-driven 6-sigma*. Explained in a simple way, 6-sigma is a tool that helps people systematically diagnose the root cause of problems that prevent Ford from achieving its goals around customer satisfaction. Ford employees have been trained in understanding and using it to identify ways to improve the customer experience.

Take, for example, customer calls. If the call is not answered in the first three rings, the customer feels dissatisfied. Six-sigma establishes that out of a million calls, all but three should be answered within three rings. It focuses attention on the whole process of receiving and answering calls.

The same approach applies to introducing new products to the market. If it can be done flawlessly, velocity, utilization of assets, and customer satisfaction all improve. A better experience for the customer encourages repeat purchases, enhances growth, and increases margins.

A third priority for Ford was to extend its premium brands (Jaguar, Aston Martin, Lincoln, Volvo, and Land Rover) worldwide, to grow the business with profitable new sales.

Mr. Nasser has chosen the business priorities he thinks will drive Ford's P-E multiple. He made these decisions based on the fundamentals of the business—cash generation, margin, velocity, return on assets, growth, and customers.

There are many things a mid-level professional might focus on to improve the P-E multiple. Say you're an engineer at Ford. Can you overcome the not-invented-here syndrome? Maybe by modifying a supplier's existing part instead of designing one yourself you can give the supplier more volume and at the same time lower the price of the part for Ford. If you save $20 million a year by so doing and you don't have to add additional shop-floor equipment, you're creating wealth for shareholders. If you come up with these solutions year after year, the P-E multiple will rise. How might this become a business priority for your department?

What if a joint effort between production, marketing, and car dealers can cut the time from when a car leaves the plant to the time it reaches the dealer and leaves the showroom floor? Think about the implications for money making, customer satisfaction, and the P-E multiple.

The opportunities exist for all employees to use their business acumen. Remember, shareholders aren't the only ones who benefit from such wealth creation. Employees, too, stand to benefit from the opportunities to earn more, grow more, and at the extreme, avoid the uncertainty of changes imposed from outside because the company has underperformed.

Part III

GETTING THINGS DONE

6

Growing People
Takes Courage

MAKING MATCHES, FIXING MISMATCHES

Each of us can practice what CEOs with superb business acumen do instinctively: cut through all the clutter using the universal laws of business, and select the right business priorities. But understanding how to make money is one thing. Making it happen, getting it done, executing it is something else. That's why CEOs with great business acumen can falter.

As any CEO knows well, in business, there are quarterly milestones but there are no finishing lines. Leaders have to deliver results day in, day out, relentlessly over a long period of time. Delivering results is what gives an organization energy, builds confidence, and generates the resources to go forward.

Assume that you've determined three or four business priorities that hang together to create a powerful money-making machine. How will you actually get the work done? Unless you're a one-man or one-woman shop, like the street vendor, you cannot personally execute them all. You need the help of other people to get them done.

Whether you're a CEO, the head of a department, or someone just starting his career, you must be a leader of the business and a leader of people. A leader of the business knows what to do. A leader of people knows how to get it done: Harness the efforts of other people, expand their personal capacity, and synchronize their efforts to get results. If you do all that, you get results. That's what I call an edge in execution.

Before we go further, let's set something straight. Being a leader of people is not the same as being a "people person." Think of someone you consider to be good with people. How would you describe that person? When I ask this question in the classes I teach, people come up with phrases like *outgoing, well-liked, lots of personality, enthusiastic, gets other people excited, charismatic.*

Personality alone is not what makes a company deliver. It takes insight into how the organization really works and how to link people's actions and decisions to the right priorities. It is this ability, in fact, that sets the superstar CEOs apart from the rest. Without it, many otherwise talented CEOs, not to mention entrepreneurs, who have superb business acumen ultimately fail in the job.

Ignore all the clutter about leadership styles and corporate culture. An edge in execution takes relentless practice, not cramming of leadership theories.

THE RIGHT PEOPLE IN THE RIGHT JOBS

There are many small shops around the world where the whole family is engaged in the business. The children help the mother and father in the shop, regardless of whether it is the best profession for them. The business may not match their natural talent, but making a living overshadows building a career by sharpening, polishing, and exploiting the natural talent. In those cases, family conflicts often arise, and the business doesn't expand much. This has been true for centuries.

Every business needs the right people in the right jobs. The modern corporation is built on the idea of professionals who use their particular talents to help the business expand. If the person making decisions is not suited to the job, the quality of the decisions is poor, and the whole company suffers. If the person is well matched to the job, she will get better and better at it, and she will get joy out of her work. The individual's capacity expands. If this is repeated throughout the company, the entire business expands.

Those leaders who deliver results consistently over a long period of time are the ones who recognize what an individual can do best. They link the business need and the person's natural talent. They take the time and effort to place individuals where their strengths can have the most impact.

Matching the person to the job begins with understanding what kinds of skills, attitudes, and aptitudes are required to accomplish the business priorities. Don't be surprised how often leaders in your work environment ignore this starting point.

If you were Sam Walton and you were trying to build a business, how would you select people to run the new stores you were building? Making money in that business means managing margin and inventory velocity and growing volume. If you can't figure out what kind of people can do that, you can forget about your dream of becoming bigger than Kmart.

Sam Walton defined the most important criterion for hiring in his business: common sense. He carefully selected people who met the criterion and developed and trained them. Employees were taught to watch sales, price, inventories, and customers like a hawk. And they had considerable autonomy to make decisions and take action.

Have you been to a Starbucks coffee shop? Did you notice its distinct ambience? What about the people who make the coffee? This could be a boring job, but they seem to enjoy the experience. Starbucks seems to have a knack for attracting and selecting people who fit the ambience. If Starbucks can't get those people and begins to deviate, fast growth could become a negative instead of a positive.

Natural talent is observable, if you take the time to watch. It's a matter of noticing which tasks come naturally to the person and energize him and others around him.

If you're in sales, you may have seen the person with the highest sales numbers get promoted to be sales manager—and totally flop. If his bosses had really observed him, they might have seen that he's an individual contributor. He thrives on getting the deal done. That's what gives him his kicks. He simply may not have the natural talent or desire to recruit other people and coach them to become superb producers. If he can't motivate other people and expand their capacity, he will not be successful in getting them to implement the business priority of increasing sales. Such a person makes a fantastic salesman but a lousy sales manager.

Consider, too, the mind-set required. Does the person have an inner drive to succeed? Is he open to change? What's the mind-set of a traditional plant manager if he's used to two inventory turns and you tell him you're going to thirty turns? What happens if he resists the idea? We've all seen people who agree to things in meetings, then go out the door and do the same old thing. If you have many of those kinds of people around, what happens to the company's ability to execute?

Sometimes when a person has worked at a company for years, the assumption is that the long time spent in the job gives her great command over the job. Yet as the real world changes, the company's business priorities shift, and the demands of the job may have changed. Recently, as Ford was making a shift to become "the world's leading consumer company providing automotive goods and services," it realized it needed certain competencies like brand management and consumer insight that many insiders had not fully developed. To achieve its new business priorities, Ford hired a lot of senior people from other companies. For example, Ford chose Wolfgang Reitzle, a former top executive from BMW, to head its premium brands group. Ford also launched several company-wide training efforts to promote consumer focus across the company.

Perhaps the best example of changing business needs is in the financial services industry. The CEOs of many of these companies are discovering that as the industry is going through global consolidation, they desperately lack leaders at all levels. Suddenly these firms have become huge and require more layers of leadership. Yet the companies do not have a pipeline of talented people who have the aptitude for leading a business on that scale. When the companies were smaller, the "excellent producers" got promoted, and somehow those individuals were expected to continue to sell while managing other people. Often, they continued to do what they loved to do—namely, sell—and neglected the managing part of the job. Their aptitude did not match the need to help others develop.

Many financial services firms have now begun to look for people who may not be the best individual contributors but have the attitude and aptitude to lead other people, who get their kicks from linking other people's energy to the business needs rather than by becoming the salesperson of the year.

Without the right people in the right jobs, a company cannot grow and thrive. In 1978, I visited a small company, then $200 million in sales, to discuss business strategy. The company was Intel, founded by three people we now call geniuses: Andy Grove, Gordon Moore, and the late Bob Noyce. These men had incredible energy, the ability to think out of the box, and the passion to create something new that would permanently alter the world and produce results for shareholders and employees. The secret of Andy Grove, who really led the company in terms of managing people and the organization, is putting the right people in the right jobs. I happened to be there when he got a call from an engineer at a large, well-known competitor. The engineer said he would take a pay cut to work for Intel because he, too, wanted to do something new and exciting. I learned later that the engineer was hired. His aptitude, attitude, and drive apparently matched the job and the needs of the company. Without people who fit, Intel could not have become the giant it is today.

DEALING WITH MISMATCHES

Think about the people around you. How many are mismatched to the job in your work environment? When the mismatch is gross, the person tends to feel insecure but may not know what to do about this and is probably uncomfortable discussing it at work. She begins to complain and drain other people's energy. The best business leaders have the confidence to confront reality, take action, and thereby plug the energy drain.

Dealing with mismatches pronto gives you an edge in execution. Yet it is the bane of many businesspeople, including many prominent CEOs I've known. Over the years I've asked many of them what was the greatest mistake they ever made in the area of people. The most common answer? "Waiting too long" to remove a direct report who was not matched to the job.

Andy Grove had a talent for hiring people who fit his fast-growing company. But as the company grew, some people could not make the grade at the new jobs. Management of Intel took appropriate action. Maybe the person better matched a job elsewhere in the company. Maybe Intel was no longer the place for him to progress. There was a certain amount of turnover of people that was driven by management. If management had ignored those mismatches, chances are we would not have heard of Intel.

Why do people so often avoid the mismatch issue? For very personal reasons. They may have a psychological commitment to the person or believe they can "bring her around," or they may simply want to avoid the possibility of a conflict. I see over and over how people prepare for these conversations, and then the day comes and they back off.

Avoiding conflict hurts the business. And nothing creates more misery for the person and for those around him. People often complain that they're not happy in their job because of the work environment. Sometimes that's true, but a mismatch in a person's natural talent and the job requirements is the real source of despair for many. Confronting and dealing with the mismatch releases energy.

Many times when an unhappy (mismatched) person is advised to leave the company, the person is at first shocked or saddened. But when he finds another company where his talents match, the energy comes alive. His wife and children see it, and happiness returns to his life. It becomes rocket fuel to progress further.

I know of one person in particular, let's call him

Paul Richards, who started out as a salesman in a $5 billion global company and soon demonstrated the talent to be a manager. He got promoted, and he flourished. He truly cared for people and was able to stretch and inspire them. Because of his success, Richards became manager of an entire country, and again, he did a superb job. From there, he was promoted to be head of Europe.

His continued success caught the interest of the CEO, to whom he was very loyal. As time went on, the CEO had a need. A key division that had grown rapidly through a series of acquisitions was beginning to fail. The person who had put the deals together was unable to execute, and as losses mounted, he had to be removed. The CEO asked Richards, then the head of Europe, to take over the failing division. Although the division was in an industry he knew nothing about, Richards accepted the challenge.

Richards dove in, but he was struggling from the start. Six months into the job, he was wallowing. With little to show for his efforts, he said he planned to change some people and bring in some consultants. After all, he was not a quitter. Meanwhile, his nonperformance was attracting his boss's attention, and as his prospects to eventually become CEO seemed to dissipate, his energy lagged.

Sensing that his career was in jeopardy, Richards resigned and took a job as CEO of another company. The new job was in an industry he knew well and called on all his natural talents. The fit was right; his confidence and energy returned. Soon after, he told me, he felt "liberated."

Another executive of a $23 billion business was a maverick at heart. The people who reported to him loved him. His peers and his bosses, however, whom he thought were incompetent, found him to be insulting. He felt he deserved to have his boss's job and eventually become the CEO. As his frustrations mounted, his bosses and peers found his behavior even more distasteful. Finally, a headhunter placed him as the CEO of a start-up company. There his natural talents and inner drive fit the job. In less than three years, he built up the company to be larger in market value than the one he had left. He is now a very high profile CEO.

COACHING

People who do well in a job also need attention. A true leader of people expands their capacity by helping them channel their skills, develop their abilities, and release their positive energy. Expanding capacity may mean giving the person a "stretch job" that will force him to develop a new skill or gain a new perspective.

How would you feel if someone gave you positive feedback on the things you're doing well and specific suggestions for building your skills? Chances are you would feel that you had a personal coach, someone who wanted to help you succeed. You would feel energized. I can tell you from experience that it works. You can do it for those who report to you, and in the process, you will expand your own capacity.

I used to hear about a guy who ran a small plastics business in Massachusetts. Every Sunday morning he would pick up the phone, call the people who reported directly to him, and discuss something he had seen in the *New York Times* that morning. This leader was using those phone calls to stimulate his people intellectually and expand their horizons. After about five Sundays, everybody was reading and discussing things they had read in the paper. They were bonding and gaining a broader view of the business landscape. (The man, by the way, was young Jack Welch early in his career.)

Maybe you think you give people feedback when you do their annual performance review. In reality, performance reviews are rarely used to develop people. Most of the time, they're simply a way to communicate a salary change based on last year's performance, or they're used to justify a promotion or demotion. That is *not* the way to help people grow and develop.

Coaching is not performance review. It's not about what someone did last year, and it's not about money. It's very personal. You're hitting the person between the eyes. You're helping him face his blind sides and learn to do things better. The feedback has to be honest and direct. No sugar coating.

Every encounter is an opportunity for coaching, and sooner is better than later. One businessman was on track to be CEO of a large company. He got raises every year and got the highest bonuses; everyone said he was fantastic; he inspired people; he always delivered on commitments. But when the board got to discussing this person, one of the directors made this comment: "He takes the hill very well, but somebody has to tell him which hill to take."

The evaluation underlying that one sentence seriously threatened the candidate's chances to become CEO. In the eyes of one of his evaluators, the person had a fatal flaw. This was the first time that flaw had ever been mentioned, and it was too late. It would have been much better for the person to have had that feedback ten years earlier, when he had time to develop.

Sometimes an adverse situation creates the opportunity for coaching. Several people told me how Jack Welch, a master at coaching, turned a botched presentation into a learning experience. The CEO was receiving a group of middle managers to review a demonstration of e-commerce. When one of the managers started to make his presentation, the equipment failed. There he stood in front of a very demanding CEO and ten of his peers. You can imagine how he felt.

What do you think the CEO did? Jack Welch immediately straightened back in his chair, looked at the group, and said, "If this happened in front of a customer, how would it have felt? Let's discuss what you would have done in that situation." Welch knew the person had rehearsed and prepared and that it could have happened to anyone. Rather than admonishing the person and creating a negative situation, he became a teacher and a coach.

Self-confident, secure leaders love to give true feedback because they know that growing people is their responsibility. By *true feedback,* I mean saying what they really think. Too often, people hesitate because they know they may be wrong, or they fear reprisal. But chances are, your instincts are correct, and they'll improve over time. I've seen numerous times that when you put experienced businesspeople around a table and they talk candidly about an individual, the judgments converge very quickly. It's not hard to zero in on the most critical thing the person needs to improve.

Some people say this kind of coaching is a good idea, but their company doesn't have the ambience for it. Still, you can start with three or four people who would be receptive to it. In one global company that never did this stuff, I saw a young manager in Uruguay sit down with people one by one and coach them. In that culture, it isn't easy to receive feedback, but he worked at it. You should see how grateful people felt toward this man. He turned the company around in six months, and his performance was so good that within a year he was identified as someone who should be watched and given new leadership opportunities. Maybe he will be a CEO someday.

Coaching on the Business Side

Most often, when leaders try to coach others, they focus only on behavior. Don't forget the business side. Can the person cut through complexity? Is the person selecting the right business priorities? Are they very specific and operational? Is she getting them done?

Here's a letter you should read. It's a disguised version of a real letter, written by a CEO ("Bob") to a division head ("Tom") of a $4 billion company. The CEO wrote the letter after a budget proposal review. Bob and Tom had had a discussion first, and then the CEO put it in writing. The company is number one in the United States and worldwide and has a good return on assets. It's a pretty good business.

July 31, 1998

Dear Tom:

Some thoughts about your budget proposal.

Your plan has to deal with lower sales and lower prices. Please get the team ahead of the curve. Don't pass up any orders. Europeans will price to employ people. You are in the midst of a fundamental change, not a cyclical one; the organization will want to make it appear temporary.

Let's allocate resources to growth markets. In resource allocation, we talk about the future, but allocate by history. Henrik needs to get European resources.

The European division needs radical change; the old guard is still there. How can we get it oriented to company goals, not regional fiefdoms? Let's drop the old national name and integrate it into the total business.

Your primary product line needs energy and fire. It has to be operated more like your newer line—product by product, leader by leader, driving the new products. It is too complex; let's simplify it.

Tom, 1998 will be your toughest year. It is a tough challenge. I'm glad you're here.

—Bob

Tom is one of the very best in the company. He's done great things. It's not easy to produce 40 percent returns, but Tom did.

Now Tom's ego is getting bruised. Bob is having to tell Tom the "how" part of his job. Apparently, Tom isn't dealing with the tough issues.

What do you see in the substance of the letter? What does Bob think Tom is missing? Change. A fundamental, structural change in the business, not a passing trend. Tom is missing it. What happens if Bob doesn't get Tom to focus on this change? How does it reflect on Bob's value as a CEO?

There's a second thing Bob is questioning. He's wondering whether Tom is devoting sufficient resources for the future. He wants Tom to look forward, not back. Bob is not just giving the guy a pat on the back and saying "nice job." He's being very specific. And you can bet he's going to follow through.

Put yourself in Tom's shoes. You know Bob values you very highly. Would this letter make you crawl into a hole? quit the job? Or might you use it as a road map? If you disagreed, maybe you'd have to go back to the boss and discuss it. Otherwise, it's a clear guide for how to develop in your career.

Now read the follow-up letter, sent six months later:

January 13, 1999

Dear Tom:

I enjoyed attending your session last week. I thought you had real energy in the room.

1998 was a pretty good year for your division. Results in Europe continue to be the disappointment and obviously must be fixed in 1999. How can I help you?

Inventories, receivables, and working capital all

showed modest improvement. As we look to 1999, there are several things I think you have to think about.

- *Global marketplace: The potential for radical change here is great. Is your team ready to make the dramatic shift in cost structure?*
- *Value products: Do we have enough emphasis on value products? That is where our program dollars have to go—now.*
- *Suppliers: The supplier management initiative must permeate the entire organization and become a way of life. Be sure you are setting the bar high enough.*
- *Developing countries: Between India and China, there are 2 billion bodies and an enormous potential market for us. I hope we can get a plan together in the first quarter, 100 percent devoted to growing these emerging markets.*

Finally, Tom, operationally for 1999, I would like you to think in terms of a total second act. The division is going through a massive transition. You must be consumed by the opportunities and the challenges you will face. You can provide great leadership; you must see the glass as half full rather than half empty.

Thanks for your help in making the supplier management initiative happen. It will make a real contribution to the total company in 1999.

—Bob

Here the CEO is talking about cost structure, product line, sales decline, growth. Out of all the complexity, he's coming up with a list of four items. He's not talking in generalities. He's not using the word *strategy*. He's getting specific. Half a year has gone by, and there hasn't been much progress. The boss is asking, "How can I help you?" In other words, he thinks help is needed.

Note that Bob's coaching in these letters is not about personal things. It's on the business side: the person's assessment of what is going on on the outside, and his ability to face the fundamental realities and needs of the business. Bob is helping Tom develop his business acumen and his judgment about people. If Tom fails to respond, he'll prove himself to be unsuited to the job.

Maybe these letters are too harsh for your junior colleagues. You can soften the language. But do the coaching on the business side. Identify just one thing about the individual that, if it were improved, would have a positive impact on the person and the group.

Coaching on Behavior

Here's an example of coaching on a specific behavior. It's a commonly observed behavior in old-line companies: A bright, hard-working, dedicated, loyal individual somehow feels constrained in a group. The person is highly respected by others, but under the pressure of group dynamics, does not feel strong enough to disagree. The person agrees to do something, knowing full well she doesn't intend to do it. One on one, the person is very open and honest and expresses herself clearly. But in the group setting, she doesn't have the courage to challenge others, and instead succumbs to commitments she cannot or does not want to meet. Such people grin and nod their head, but as soon as the meeting is over, the agreement is broken.

This weakness is debilitating to the individual and the group. It causes decisions to have to be revisited and reworked, and slows the group's progress. It may well prevent the group from achieving its business priorities. It's the leader's job to identify this weakness, help the individual become aware of it, and coach the person on how to overcome it.

Or take the example of the CEO of a large technology company headquartered outside the United States coaching one of his direct reports, who is new to the industry. The CEO writes a letter full of compliments for the first two pages. Then come the areas for improvement:

. . . It will be important for you to enhance your performance in the following areas:

1. *You should delve more deeply into the operational details of your businesses. Whether it is service levels or capital expenditures, you must be versed in the inner workings of each business and hold managers strictly accountable for high achievement. While you came from outside the industry, you are a quick study. It will serve you better to have a stronger knowledge base.*
2. *Sometimes you are too sympathetic to people and accept plans or performance from them that are, in fact, substandard. Raise your standards. Always*

keep your standards at or above what we must achieve to propel the company forward as a global company of excellence.

The CEO is basically saying that the person is being too nice. The person's behavior is getting in the way of results. Maybe he's unsure of himself because he's still learning the industry. The CEO is telling him to take charge and hold people accountable. Now this leader knows he has support in dealing with the people issues.

I know of another businessman who was described as fabulous, brilliant, a visionary, very committed. This man was told by his CEO that he was not tough enough to cut his losses. What does that mean? Maybe he had a fear of admitting failure and was holding on too long to a business that was losing money, or maybe he was continuing to pour money into a failing project, or maybe he was not facing up to the fact that a key person he had hand-picked was not matched to the job.

If the person gets the feedback right away and makes the correction, the company will perform better. It's an edge in execution.

7

Making Groups Decisive

DESIGNING SOCIAL OPERATING
MECHANISMS[SM]

Talking about individuals does not fully capture the reality of an organization. Draw on your experience. What's missing? All the stuff that connects people to each other. Even if you have the right people in the right jobs, unless you synchronize their efforts and link them to the business priorities, you do not have an edge in execution. The money making doesn't happen.

A synchronized organization is like a champion rowing team—people working together with a certain rhythm that allows the group to do things the individuals could not do. Synchronization expands the capacity of the whole group.

For a shopkeeper whose family works with him, synchronization is not a big issue. His sons and daughters may not have precisely the talents the business needs, but they may coordinate their efforts quite naturally. In a small organization, everyone knows every-thing that's going on. People overhear each other on the phone; they go to lunch together. They automatically adjust to each other and make necessary trade-offs. If there's confusion, they talk.

But as an organization grows and you have dozens, if not hundreds, of people working together, synchro-nization becomes a greater challenge. To divide respon-sibilities, you create an organizational structure. The moment you create that structure, the social interaction in the organization changes. Often, the information that flows from one part of the organization to another gets clogged or distorted. The bigger the company, the harder it is for people to share information, make joint decisions, and adjust their priorities. Decision making slows. The edge in execution gets blunted.

The lack of synchronization explains why so many small shopkeepers and vendors never expand. They do not know how to create mechanisms that bring people together in a meaningful way, expand their individual capacity, and build the capacity of the total business.

An edge in execution requires mechanisms that syn-chronize individual contributors, what I have begun to call "Social Operating Mechanisms." Social Operating Mechanisms are critical to an edge in execution.

WAL-MART'S SOCIAL OPERATING MECHANISM

Sam Walton created a Social Operating Mechanism for which I think he would deserve a Nobel Prize in busi-ness (if there were such a thing).

In the early 1990s, every Monday to Wednesday, some thirty regional managers went out to visit nine Wal-Mart stores and six of their competitors' stores. They gathered a basket of goods and compared the prices. In 1991, Wal-Mart had a policy about having prices that were 8 percent lower than those of major competitors in the area, and this weekly visiting was their way of knowing that the strategy of lower prices was actually being executed.

What are the regional managers observing if they're doing the job right? Not just prices. They're seeing the merchandise, how it is presented, what consumers are buying, what the stores look like, what the ambience is, what new practices competitors are using, and how employees are behaving.

Go back to the fundamentals. Remember consumers. Who are they and what are they buying? Is your business offering sustainable for the future? You assess this through competitive analysis, which for Wal-Mart was going on constantly.

Notice how many filters there are at Wal-Mart between the regional managers and where the action is: zero. What is the value of zero information filters? Time and quality. Zero delay. Zero distortion. Zero distrust. And what is happening to the honing of the senses? The skill improves with practice.

On Thursday mornings, Sam Walton conducted a four-hour session with a group of some fifty managers. They included the regional managers who visited stores, buyers, logistics people, and advertising people. Maybe it would come out in the Thursday morning meeting that one region needs a hundred thousand more grosses of sweaters on the shelf by Tuesday. By the way, those sweaters are not moving in the Northeast. It's not cold enough or whatever. Maybe inventory is getting adjusted.

Information is being exchanged and integrated, decisions are made, and every participant is getting a total picture of the business and a feel for the competition that is no more than one week old. People are acting on unfiltered information gathered directly from consumers and frontline employees.

Sam Walton's Social Operating Mechanism brought his priorities from the 50,000-foot level to the 50-foot level, where the synchronization had to take place. At the same time, the accountability was built in. If someone wasn't readily participating in the discussion, this was very visible.

Wal-Mart is truly a consumer-oriented company. But the point is not to copy Wal-Mart's Social Operating Mechanisms. You have to detect for yourself where information sharing and trade-offs are critical and then design Social Operating Mechanisms that are right for your company.

DESIGNING SOCIAL OPERATING MECHANISMS

Think about how you synchronize and integrate your efforts with those of other people at work. Chances are you do much of it through meetings. But as a Social Operating Mechanism, most meetings are weak. The wrong people attend; the dialogue is fragmented; there's no leadership; no decisions get made; there's no follow-through. Sometimes meetings are used to display a deck of useless slides. Sometimes they become a forum to blame people for not doing the right things.

Find a better way. Do the work on the business side first. Set the priorities. Then take the time to design Social Operating Mechanisms, whether a conference call or a fifteen-minute meeting, that gets information flowing and the right people talking. Think of the characteristics of Wal-Mart's Social Operating Mechanism: simultaneous flow of information, informal dialogue, zero filters, frequency, boundarylessness.

Other companies have created similar mechanisms. One business unit at GE, for instance, regularly uses conference calls for "quick market intelligence," a technique patterned on Wal-Mart's Social Operating Mechanism. The GE business unit saw the value of simultaneous communication, but because of its wide geographic spread, managers could not attend face-to-face meetings with great frequency. QMI brings them together by video and phone. Now, at least once every two weeks, a dialogue takes place among some fifty people from around the world—India, France, Japan, the United Kingdom, Australia, Chicago, New York.

The frequency and rhythm of the information exchange keeps all QMI participants, no matter where they are in the hierarchy or the globe, up to date on what's happening with customers, competitors, and technology worldwide. That way, they can better anticipate price changes and new issues that are arising. All fifty people have the same view of the outside world.

As they set their priorities three months out, they are synchronized.

This unit of GE has even developed certain guidelines for making QMI calls effective: Discussion questions should be specific and simple enough to be answered in two minutes; all participants should be put at ease and encouraged to contribute; meetings should be short, so people don't lose interest; information should be processed along the way and summarized at the end.

GE's QMI gets results because it helps people exchange the information and ideas needed to make the right trade-offs and the best decisions. People share information and come to a common conclusion. Most conflicts are brought to the surface and resolved promptly. This is a crucial building block for achieving speed at GE.

The frequency and rhythm of QMI creates a social cohesion that makes people comfortable crossing organizational boundaries between conference calls. Following one such conference call, a GE scheduler, several layers removed from the vice president of manufacturing, felt comfortable calling the VP directly instead of going through the formal hierarchy. Communication was flowing; boundaries were breaking.

A Social Operating Mechanism can be as simple as a letter or report from the CEO that opens the information flow and creates new behavior. At another company, the new CEO knew that employees were basically well skilled and well meaning, yet the company hadn't been earning a profit. Rework and high costs were killing the business. In his first thirty days on the job, he introduced a profit-sharing plan and made sure that everyone understood how it worked. Then he started issuing weekly reports on the three items that were the biggest money guzzlers: the total number of employees, the amount of rework, and damaged goods.

One thirty-year veteran was shocked by the reports. He said: "I didn't know we weren't making money. I could cut costs in half if you'd let me." The employee explained his ideas, and they made sense. Four months later, the plant was profitable. The weekly reports gave everyone a common view of the business and helped channel the company's human energy toward the business priorities.

Designing Social Operating Mechanisms is a leadership task, not a human resources department task. Use your creativity and take it on as a personal challenge.

8

What to Do
and How to Do It

An edge in execution comes from having the right people in the right jobs, synchronizing their efforts, and releasing and channeling their energy toward the right set of business priorities. It takes business acumen to select the right business priorities. It takes insight into people and the organization to get the energy aligned.

You can give your department, business unit, or company an edge in execution by developing your business acumen and your judgment about people. The combination is irrefutably successful in the real world of business. Jack Welch is an obvious master, but if you look below the surface at the behavior of other successful CEOs, you will observe a common pattern. CEOs who deliver results have mastered both the business side and the people side. Unless the CEO masters both parts of the leadership equation, the company cannot continue to deliver results and succeed.

Let's take a close look at Dick Brown, who became CEO of EDS, the giant information technology services company, in January 1999. EDS was the brainchild of Ross Perot, who had founded the information technology outsourcing industry. It was acquired by General Motors in 1984 and spun off from GM in 1996. After the spin-off, EDS missed its earnings commitments for several quarters. By the late 1990s, it was in a slump, and the board of directors was under enormous pressure to turn the situation around. They hired Dick Brown, then CEO of Cable & Wireless, to lead EDS.

Even before Dick Brown arrived on the scene, he began to immerse himself in the complexity of the business. The information technology services business is inherently complex, and that complexity was compounded by the fact that the company was huge and global, with about $17 billion in revenue and 125,000 employees in 46 countries. The company also happened to be at the crossroads of fundamental changes in technology and was trying to adjust to the business opportunities presented by the explosion of the Internet. Brown pored through the volumes of data the board had sent—current and historical financial statements, competitive data, market analyses, forecasts, and lists of contracts won or lost. As soon as he arrived at the organization, he made the rounds to leaders throughout the company.

Dick Brown happens to be one of those businessmen who thinks like a street vendor. Within sixty days, using his business acumen, he cut through the complexity to the fundamentals of the business—that by now familiar list: cash generation, margin, velocity, return on assets, growth, and customers (EDS refers to them as clients).

Here's what he found: Although EDS had a great history, it had lost its lead to IBM in recent years. While the industry was growing at 15 percent a year, EDS's revenue was growing in the 9 to 10 percent range—slower than the market. Margins had been slipping for several years, and return on assets was in a steady decline. The company had been missing its promises to Wall Street, and its stock price had been cut in half during a time when the S&P 500 was on the rise.

Stepping back from his diagnosis of the business, Brown had to consider how they could improve the money making. EDS's cash situation was fine. Its revenue growth and margins were problematic. EDS's weak stock price and P-E multiple of 17 reflected investors' perception that the company was not on a growth trajectory.

Pinpointing the trouble spots drove the search for the right business priorities. Several important insights came from group discussions: 20 percent of the sales force hadn't sold any new business in the prior nine to twelve months, and many others had left in disgust. Also, incentives were geared to reward big, long-term contracts, not necessarily profitable ones. Business units had duplicate resources, and the central technology unit was underutilized.

These insights helped Dick Brown identify a set of business priorities, including:

- Growing revenue from sources other than GM at or above the market growth rate.
- Improving client service levels.
- Reducing costs by $1 billion and thus improving margin.
- Achieving double-digit margins by the end of 2000.

If creating such a clear, simple list seems like a great accomplishment in itself, you're right. Not every business leader has the business acumen to get this far. But remember, this is only part of the winning formula. Dick Brown then had to get people energized and aligned. All along, he had been taking stock of whether he had the right people in the right jobs around him. Indeed, some of the direct reports he had inherited were up to the challenges. They had simply not been given clear priorities before. Others, it turned out, lacked either the aptitude or attitude. Brown mustered the courage to address the mismatches. He did not delay taking action. He moved fast.

Next, Brown began to create the Social Operating Mechanisms that would make the business priorities achievable. One of the most significant of these is the monthly "performance call," a conference call that includes about a hundred top business leaders at EDS around the world. Dick Brown conducts the call, with the help of the CFO and the president and chief operating officer. During the call, each unit's monthly and year-to-date results are discussed. The subject matter alone is far different from what these people had focused on in the past.

At the start, most of the participants really didn't have a sense of urgency about the business elements of revenue growth, margin, and market share. Brown used the conference calls to emphasize their importance. He opens each call by summarizing highlights of the month or year to date. The CFO then reviews profit for the month and year and how it compares with the targets. Next the president and COO goes through the sales results. Sharing results openly and frequently creates a kind of built-in accountability. It is immediately clear who is doing well and who needs help. In the question-and-answer period that follows, Brown sets the tone for the organization by ensuring that the dialogue is candid, concise, and constructive. If performance falls significantly short, he follows up with those leaders afterward.

The listening, learning, and coaching on the business side takes place within the Social Operating Mechanism. At the same time, the common goals are reinforced, and decisions get made.

Other Social Operating Mechanisms were established elsewhere in the organization and help the senior team identify opportunities to achieve the business priorities. The "senior leadership meeting," for example, brings the top 130 or so executives together in one place three times a year. The purpose is to discuss the business as a whole, to practice working as a team, and to emphasize through candid, constructive dialogue a new way of working together to get results.

A third mechanism is the biweekly e-mails Dick Brown sends to everyone at EDS, addressed "To the EDS Worldwide Team." Written in a direct, informal tone, the e-mails acknowledge particular accomplishments and discuss where the company stands in terms of the business priorities. In one e-mail, Brown wrote, "I will continue to reinforce that we are a growth business. To all of you in the marketplace—*continue to stoke our engines of EDS growth.* This must be 'profitable' growth—growth with the margins we need to satisfy our investors and that are fair to our clients."

Once the right perspectives were shared and brought to bear on EDS's problems, the solutions became more obvious. Productivity, for instance, meant eliminating redundant business functions. Maybe EDS needed to reorganize itself to share its resources more effectively. Growing sales meant serving clients better. How could a reorganization improve client satisfaction? The answer was to replace the forty-some business units with four lines of business designed around major market sectors. The biweekly e-mails prompted many readers to suggest other cost-cutting ideas, from slashing the corporate air force to cutting first-class travel.

By the end of 1999, EDS had in fact cut $1 billion in costs and was on its way to streamlining its operations and becoming more client oriented. It had removed nonperformers from the sales force and hired new people with proven track records. The company had renewed its focus on attracting and retaining talent, and growth, client satisfaction, and accountability were taking root. Since then, EDS has continued to strengthen.

The point is not to sing the praises of one individual leader. What Dick Brown has accomplished at EDS others have accomplished at other companies. But none of these successes could have been achieved without business acumen on the one hand, and leadership of people and the organization on the other. Business acumen provides the road map and clarity. But unless you want to be a one-man or one-woman shop, you must learn how to link business priorities and people.

You don't have to be a CEO to practice being a leader of the business and a leader of people. Say you're a product line manager. The thought process is the same. Assess the fundamentals of the product line and consider why they are going one way or the other and how they might be improved. When you know what must be done, think about the people around you. Do they have the skills and talents required? How can you coach them? What kind of Social Operating Mechanisms might speed the flow of information and decisions?

Part IV

YOUR PERSONAL AGENDA

9

Your Part in the Big Picture

REKINDLING THE SPIRIT
OF THE LEMONADE STAND

By now you should be speaking the universal language of business. No matter what level you are in the organization, you should have a shopkeeper's view of your company's total business and be wrestling with the inherent complexity. You should also have an appreciation for how money making is valued by the stock market.

You are probably reading this book because you want to be a leader. How can you as a leader use your business acumen to improve the business, keeping in mind cash generation, return on assets, growth, and customers? How can you get results by tapping every individual's intellectual energy?

Link your own priorities to the big picture. If you're in human resources, for example, you can help people break out of their chimneys and coordinate efforts with people elsewhere in the company to help ensure that the company has the right people in the right jobs. The wrong person in the job can have a tremendously damaging effect on cash generation, margin, velocity, return on assets, and growth.

If you're in information technology, maybe you can create links with customers and suppliers so your company can collaborate more easily. An attorney in the office of the general counsel can help by keeping up to date with legislative changes globally and staying alert for new opportunities that might arise as a result. Those in finance can help with many kinds of decisions—whether to add capacity, how to improve pricing for better margins, and the like—by providing accurate and timely information. Finance can also be a partner in analyzing the most promising growth opportunities.

But I hope you are convinced that professional excellence alone is not sufficient. As you learn to think like the street vendor, you will become a businessperson first. Your perspective will expand beyond a functional or departmental view to a total business view. As your view expands, your thinking may become more creative. You will feel empowered to ask questions in any meeting, without fear of hierarchy or embarrassment. Take the lead in your group in relating discussions to the universal laws of business.

Maybe you can break new ground by coming up with a creative new idea that relates to the overall business. At Ford, for example, e-commerce tools are being leveraged to better access the market for materials and services. Ford can solicit bids from suppliers and conclude the bidding process in one to two hours. Cost savings average 20 to 30 percent.

Maybe you can help by simply reframing an issue, bringing the underlying assumptions to the surface and challenging them. What does it mean to reframe an issue? Say you work for a consumer electronics company and someone is arguing that you have to cut costs on a particular product. Put on your businessperson's hat and ask what customer needs are not being met. If you can meet them, would that create value and boost demand for the product? If so, how would that affect utilization of manufacturing capacity? Are there features that customers don't care much about and can be eliminated to reduce cost? In other words, broaden the range of options for meeting the money-making criteria.

ASSESS THE TOTAL BUSINESS

Every company faces challenges. Begin by making sure you understand the ones your company faces.

- What were your company's sales during the last year?
- Are sales growing, declining, or flat? What do you think about this growth picture?
- What is your company's profit margin? Is it growing, declining, or flat?
- How does your margin compare with competitors'? How does it compare with those of other industries?
- Do you know your company's inventory velocity? its asset velocity?

- What is your company's return on assets? If you know the margin and the asset velocity, do the math: $R = M \times V$.
- Is your company's cash generation increasing or decreasing? Why is it going one way or the other?
- Is your company gaining or losing against the competition?

Recap the fundamentals for your company. Don't let hierarchy and chimneys get in the way of understanding the essence of your company's business. Step back and get a total picture of the business. Does your assessment match the view you're hearing from senior management? Are there questions you should ask, or suggestions you can make? Should you test your assessment with others around you?

CUT THROUGH COMPLEXITY

Now think about the broader context your company operates in. What are the external realities of your particular business? Make a list of all the things that could affect your company's money-making ability.

- Is there excess capacity in the industry?
- Is the industry consolidating?
- Do you face stiff pricing competition?
- Might your business be affected by currency fluctuations or changes in interest rates one way or the other?
- Are you facing new competitors?

- What is happening in e-commerce? How might that affect the company?

Chances are, your list of external considerations will be long, the complexity great. Before you read on, decide which factors you think are significant. Are some of them connected? Are there certain trends? Don't expect this to come easily. It takes practice to cut through the complexity, and you may not have all the information you need. You may have to ask for it.

Before you read on, take the time to determine a couple of patterns or trends you think are important, and write them here:

1.

2.

PROVIDE FOCUS

As you cut through the complexity, you will get a clear fix on what is happening in the real world. Then you must determine the three or four business priorities for your group, department, or business unit. How will they combine to enhance money making?

Some of you have the intellectual capacity to cut through complexity but are indecisive or afraid of being wrong. Can you wait until all the facts are in and the picture is clearer? Here's the rub: You make a bet even when you don't make a bet! That is, by not choosing to do anything different, you are choosing the status quo.

Have the courage and conviction to provide focus for your area. You have to decide what your department, division, or business unit must do and what it must stop doing. You have to determine the business priorities, and those priorities have to be consistent and aligned with the corporate goals. You can't have too many, you can't keep changing, and you have to communicate them clearly and repeatedly. If your business acumen is any good (of course you'll keep improving it), you'll understand why that particular combination of business priorities will make money.

Don't get swept up in grandiose visions of what you want to accomplish. Bring the vision below the 50,000-foot level. You should be able to explain what you need to do in clear, simple terms, and you should be able to explain how it will improve money making.

Apply your common sense. Your business sense. You will be surprised how many good ideas you can generate. Write your business priorities here:

1.

2.

3.

4.

HELP PEOPLE EXPAND THEIR ABILITIES AND SYNCHRONIZE THEIR WORK EFFORTS

Consider the individuals who report to you and others you interact with in your everyday work life. You don't have to be a top executive to develop other people's talents and match them to the job or to design Social Operating Mechanisms that make groups of people function better. Find ways to share unfiltered information simultaneously and to bring conflicts to the surface.

Think about the match between individuals you supervise and their jobs:

- What are the two or three non-negotiable requirements of the job now and two years out?

- What are the two or three things you would call the individual's natural talents and drive?
- What is the one major blind side of the person that might prevent him or her from growing further?
- How can you help coach this person?

Then focus on a work group, team, or the organization as a whole and ask:

- Are ideas and information exchanged openly and filter-free?
- What is the speed of decision making?
- What is the quality of decisions?
- Do decisions stick, or are they often revisited and reworked?
- Do people find meetings constructive and energy-building or destructive and energy-draining?

BE A LEADER

Be a leader of the business. With the command and urgency of a street vendor, pick the three or four items you and those reporting to you should focus on. Don't try to cover the waterfront, don't keep changing your mind, and don't back away from the challenge. Make the priorities known by repeating them often.

Be a leader of people. Go beyond the street vendor to build an organization that can execute the business priorities. Find the right people for the job, and take personal responsibility for releasing their energy and developing their skills. When someone's aptitude or attitude gets in the way of execution, address the issue. Don't forget to help others develop their own business acumen.

Synchronize the organization. Link people's efforts to the business priorities. Find mechanisms that increase the information flow and coordinate people's work. Make the group more decisive. Build the team.

Start at the beginning. Return to your earliest experience in business, when you understood the nucleus of delivering newspapers or selling lemonade or whatever it was you did to make money. Expand on your business acumen by practicing it in more complex situations. Don't be afraid to make mistakes and learn from them. Make judgments that reflect business acumen, and share your knowledge.

Don't let this book become an intellectual exercise. Before you close the cover, start thinking in concrete terms. Be prepared to answer the inevitable question: What are you going to do to help your company's money making in the next sixty to ninety days? Be a part of it. Let the excitement begin.

Index

ABOUT THE AUTHOR

For more than thirty years, **Ram Charan** has been coaching and advising some of the world's most successful business leaders on a range of business issues, from strategy to leadership development. Among senior executives at many Fortune 500 companies, he is highly sought for his practical, real-world advice. He is also highly sought as a teacher. He has taught thousands of managers throughout the world, including thirty years at GE's Crotonville Institute, and MBA, doctoral, and advanced management programs at Harvard Business School, Northwestern University's Kellogg School, Columbia, and Wharton. He earned Best Teacher awards from GE, the Kellogg School, and Wharton's Life Insurance Institute and was named in *Business Week*'s top ten teachers for in-house executive education. He is the author of *Boards at Work* (on Heidrick and Struggles's list of top ten leadership books) and *"Action, Urgency, and Excellence."* He is coauthor of numerous books, including *Every Business Is a Growth Business* and *E-Board Strategies*. His articles have appeared in a wide range of publications, including *Harvard Business Review, Fortune,* the *Financial Times, USA Today,* and *Director's Monthly*. He holds DBA and MBA (with High Distinction, Baker Scholar) degrees from Harvard Business School, is on the board of directors of Austin Industries, and is a fellow of the National Academy of Human Resources. He is based in Dallas, Texas.